THE SATANIC CULT

DESCRIPTION ET FIGVRE DV SABBAT DES SORCIERS.

Il faut mettre cette Figure au Diſcours 4. du 2. Liure, entre les pages 118. & 119.

A Satan eſt dans vne Chaire doree en forme de Bouc, qui preſche auec cinq cornes, ayant la cinquieſme allumee pour allumer toutes les chandelles & feux du Sabbat.

B La Roine du Sabbat couronnee à dextre, & vne moins fauorie à ſeneſtre.

C Au deſſous de ſa chaire, eſt vne Sorciere qui luy preſente vn enfant qu'elle a ſeduit.

D Voila les Conuiues de l'aſſemblee, ayant chacune vn Demon pres d'elle: Et en ce feſtin, ne ſe ſert autre viande, que charoignes, chair de pendus, cœurs d'enfans non baptiſez, & autres animaux immondes, du tout hors du commerce & vſage des Chreſtiens, le tout incipide & ſans ſel.

E En ce feſtin ne ſont admis, ces ſpectateurs, qui ſont pluſieurs poures Sorcieres reiettees aux recoings, & qui n'oſent s'approcher des grandes ceremonies.

F Apres la pance vient la danſe: car apres auoir eſté repeus de viandes, ou fugitiues, ou illuſoires, ou tres-pernicieuſes & abominables; chaque Demon meine celle qui eſtoit pres de luy à table, au deſſous de cet arbre maudit, & là le premier ayant le viſage tourné vers le rond de la danſe, & le ſecond en dehors, & les autres ainſi enſuiuant tout de meſme, ils danſent, trepignent & tripudient, auec les plus indecens & ſales mouuemens qu'ils peuuent.

G Ce ſont les ioüeurs d'inſtrumens, & le concert de Muſique, au chant & harmonie de laquelle ils danſent & ſautent.

H Au deſſous ſe void vne troupe de femmes & filles qui danſent toutes le viſage en dehors le rond de la danſe.

I Voila la Chaudiere ſur le feu pour faire toute ſorte de poiſon, ſoit pour faire mourir & malcficier les hommes, ſoit pour gaſter le beſtail; l'vne tient les ſerpens & crapaux en main, & l'autre leur couppe la teſte, & les eſcorche, puis les iette dans la chaudiere.

K Pendant cet entretien pluſieurs Sorcieres arriuent au Sabbat ſur des baſtons & balais, d'autres ſur des Boucs accompagnees des enfans qu'elles ont enleué & ſuborné, leſquels elles viennent offrir à Satan: D'autres partant du Sabbat, & tranſportees en l'air, s'en vont ſur la mer ou ailleurs exciter des orages & tempeſtes.

L Ce ſont les grands Seigneurs & Dames, & autres gens riches & puiſſans, qui traictent les grands affaires du Sabbat, où ils paroiſſent voilez, & les femmes auec des maſques, pour ſe tenir touſiours à couuert & incogneus.

M Pres de ce ruiſſeau ſont les petits enfans, leſquels auec des verges & houſſines blanches, eſloignez des ceremonies, gardent chacun les troupeaux des crapaux de celles qui ont accouſtumé les mener au Sabbat.

Outre ce, il y a pluſieurs autres choſes que la petiteſſe de ceſte figure n'a peu ſouffrir, qui ſe pourront entendre commodément par le Diſcours du Sabbat, qui eſt au Diſcours 4. du Liure ſecond.

The Witches' Sabbath, illustration from Pierre de Lancre, *Tableau de l'inconstance des mauvais anges et démons* (Paris, 1613)

The Satanic Cult

GERHARD ZACHARIAS

Translated by
Christine Trollope

London
GEORGE ALLEN & UNWIN
Boston Sydney

First published in English in 1980

GEORGE ALLEN & UNWIN LTD
40 Museum Street, London WC1A 1LU

British Library Cataloguing in Publication Data

Zacharias, Gerhard
The Satanic cult.
1. Satanism
I. Title
133.4'22 BF1548 79-41557

ISBN 0-04-133008-0

Typeset in 11 on 12 point Baskerville by Northampton Phototypesetters Ltd
and printed in Great Britain
by Biddles Ltd, Guildford, Surrey

PREFACE

Since this book first appeared in German in 1964, developments have occurred which can largely be explained by reference to the tradition of Satan worship.

'All around us, beatniks, *Gammler*, *voyous*, *provos*, "happeners", *capelloni*, hippies, flower children, revolutionary students or Vietniks and Peaceniks have called in question the existing order of things, aroused the apathetic and given those in authority a great deal to worry about. The year 1968 was a great year for youth in protest. In England and America they began to form their own culture in opposition to that of their elders. All over the world they battered down the doors of universities and government offices. In France, risings and counter-risings broke out; and everywhere the dry bones of democracy were brought to life, and the Establishment was forced to lay bare the means wherewith it ruled.'[1] The social revolution became to some extent a sexual revolution, with the name of Wilhelm Reich emblazoned on its banner.[2] Without any doubt this world-wide protest is a complete reaction to the traditional cultures of the Christian world. Occasionally it is directly or indirectly linked with Satan worship, but on the whole it remains on this side of Satanism, which is why its consequences are so unpredictable.

The directly Satanic aspects of the modern subculture are easily identified and recognised as epigonous. The best known is the Hollywood group of hippies led by Charles Manson (who according to press reports sometimes called himself 'Satan') which was responsible for the murder of at least five people, including the film star Sharon Tate. Manson had joined the 'Church of Scientology of California' (and later a splinter group from it), the head of which had been inspired by Aleister Crowley among others (see p. 146f).[3] This present-day Satanism also includes, for example, certain cases of sacrilege,[4] and some innocuous imitations of the type of a 'Swabian Black Mass'.[5] Roman Polanski's film *Rosemary's Baby* (1967) helped to make the subject known to a wider audience.

But themes from Satan worship can also enter in a more indirect way into literary or artistic revolt. They can be found in a rudimentary form in the revolutionary street theatre.[6] An outstanding example is Otto Muehl, whose *Materialaktion* in Brunswick in December 1969 called forth an intense reaction from the Press.[7]

The fact that modern subculture has a marked tendency to go beyond the dualistic tradition of Christianity (Wassermann's invocation in the introductory scene of the musical *Hair* can be taken as a symbol of this; the problem of the use of hallucinogens must also be seen in this context) raises a question that needs to be seriously considered.

The psychoanalyst Wolfgang Loch has shown in his work *Uber die Zusammenhänge zwischen Partnerschaft, Struktur und Mythos*[8] that the symbiotic relationship between mother and child in early infancy is characterised by the exclusion of evil; where there are two partners, both are good, and evil remains 'outside'. When the relationship is extended to take in a third person – the father – and the oedipal situation comes into play, evil must perforce be taken into account, and 'the way out by splitting off the bad object or the bad self' is 'barred'.[9] As it is impossible to love bad objects or take them as models, separation from evil naturally postulates that it should be recognised as a part of one's own psyche and consequently integrated into the personality.

The dualism of Christianity, together with Satanism, corresponds to this relationship of three persons; but in this case the process of integration of evil has not taken place, having been blocked by special defence systems (see Chapter 1.3). The modern subculture – particularly under the influence of elements of Indian religion and meditation – tends to return to the dual pattern, and is thus regressive in nature. It is, in other words, a symbiotic fantasy with corresponding feelings of omnipotence. As an underground poem puts it '. . . to be really just that:/Invisible and in complete control of everything'.[10]

A non-regressive solution to the problem of evil would be provided by what Michael Balint calls 'genital love'.[11] Unlike the pregenitally determined forms of love, in which the evasion of the problem is paid for by definite loss of autonomy, genital love needs constantly to dominate. This means that the ego is continually on the watch, and only in rare moments is there 'a brief return to a perfect unity of the microcosm and the macrocosm'.[12] Present-day subculture has something that transcends the traditional Christian dualism. Is this simply a step back, or could it be the reflection of a forward movement? This is the burning question of our time.

G.Z.

CONTENTS

LIST OF PLATES

LINE DRAWINGS

AUTHOR'S NOTE

I would like to express my gratitude to the publishers, George Allen & Unwin, for making an English edition possible, and also to Dr Christine Trollope, the translator, for the skill with which she has performed a far from easy task. My thanks also to Dr A. A. Barb, of The Warburg Institute, London, for his kind suggestions and to Mrs Hildegard Barth-Chapman, who helped me greatly in reading through the English version.

My commentary on the texts has been slightly abridged, but also contains some additions. The original-language versions of the texts reproduced may be found in the German edition, *Satanskult und Schwarze Messe*, 2nd edition 1970, published by Limes Verlag, Munich (formerly of Wiesbaden).

INTRODUCTION

This book deals with an essential aspect of 'Satanism', which the *Enciclopedia Cattolica* defines as 'The state of being satanic, that is, subject to the actions of Satan, or consecrated to the Enemy of God, or pervaded with his spirit'.[1] The opposition of God and Satan is one of the fundamentals of Christianity, and thus Satanism is directly related to the Christian tradition. In fact it is the central theme of the 'dark side' of Christianity.[2]

Satan worship, in which Satanism shows itself particularly strongly, is a direct antithesis of the Christian cult. As the latter centres on the mass, so the cult of Satan culminates in a perversion of the Roman liturgy; towards the end of the nineteenth century[3] this became generally known as the black mass. The adjective 'black' was chosen partly because of its symbolism and partly because the wafers were sometimes made of slices of turnip dyed black, or of other black material.

For reasons that will be discussed in the first part of this book, Christianity connects the worship of Satan with the Dionysian cult, the cult of the great Earth-mother,[4] and the sex act. These three have accordingly become special areas of Satanism and thus of Satan worship. So the field of our research extends over such subjects as religious ecstasy, witchcraft and religious orgies. In some cases Dionysiac, matriarchal or sexual rites *per se*, that is without any expressed purpose, have features that appear Satanic or at least in revolt against official Christianity. We shall discuss these borderline cases also.

The complex of facts that forms the subject-matter of this book has been up to now a kind of stepchild of traditional scholarship. There exists a reasonable number of well documented and valuable works on witchcraft in the narrower sense, black magic, Satanism in literature, and so on; but with few exceptions Satan worship and the black mass are favourite subjects for sentimental, tendentious or crudely sensational outpourings. None of the publications on this theme gives much in the way of source material.

This contribution to the phenomenology of religion aims to provide a starting-point for further discussion of a hitherto relatively neglected branch of the subject, which deserves attention for a variety of reasons. In order that the facts in question may be seen as far as possible 'in the round', and to give the reader a chance to form his own judgement, essential sources dating from all periods are given in the main body of the work; these documents, together with illustrations, will serve as a basis for interpretation. The introductory section fixes the limits within which the Satan cult is to be understood. The concluding section is concerned with queries and problems arising from the phenomena discussed.

The author follows the principles developed by the Dutch authority on comparative religion, G. van der Leeuw (1890–1950) for his research on the phenomenology of religion.[5] 'Phenomenology seeks *phenomena*. But a phenomenon means *that which appears*. . . . A phenomenon is not produced by the subject, still less substantiated or proved. Its whole essence depends on the fact that it appears – appears to "someone". If this "someone" begins to talk about what has appeared, that is phenomenology.'[6] According to van der Leeuw the task of phenomenology is first to name the phenomena and show them as they appear on the surface, then to explain them, analyse their structure, place them in a wider context, and finally to draw conclusions that can stand as evidence. The phenomenology of religion is not to be equated with religious history, theology, or the philosophy, psychology or sociology of religion. What does this mean as far as our study is concerned?

First, it was never my intention to write a history of the Satan cult and the black mass, although the material to be phenomenologically explained is arranged in chronological order and sometimes placed in a historical setting. The reader should not, therefore, expect the work to be historically complete (in any case the enormous amount of material would make this quite impossible in one book). The choice of texts, illustrations and historical details depends rather on the information they contribute; I have given only as much as is of value for the phenomenological work, and sufficient to enable the reader to verify and understand the phenomena in question. As this book does not purport to be a piece of historical research, the question of the historicity of the facts discussed has not been gone into as closely as might otherwise have been required. Apart from the fact that much of this particular subject remains obscure, and in places it is impossible to draw a line between imagination and deliberate falsehood, the problem of physical reality is irrelevant in phenomenology, inasmuch as even imaginings have their own reality, existing on the same level as 'factual' events.

It is important, next, to distinguish the work in hand from theology and philosophy. Theology is about God. 'In phenomenology God is neither subject nor object; he must be a phenomenon, that is to say, appear.'[7] So if we speak of God, of the divine or of theological conceptions, we mean simply a manifestation, something that appears; divine reality itself persists in the *Epoche*, the 'binding force'.[8] Speculations of a philosophical kind are also excluded, for the '*Epoche*' comes into play here also. In order to obviate misunderstandings – particularly on the theological side – we must emphasise at this point that the term 'dualistic', which is used throughout, is to be understood in a phenomenological but not in a theological or philosophical sense.

Nor is this purely a psychology of religion. Where the divine and the human are intertwined, religious psychology, to attain its ends, separates out the human part, and even there considers only the intellectual aspect. The danger of confusing our point of view with that of the psychology of religion is the greater because readers who are accustomed to think along the lines of traditional Christianity will tend to jump to the conclusion that the Satan cult and the black mass are simply a product of diseased minds under the influence of the enemies of religion, without seeing that there may also be an element of the divine concealed within them. I should like to ask these readers to suspend judgement as otherwise the way to the natural phenomenological conclusion is blocked.

In our time the traditional type of psychology of religion has moved more and more towards the interpretation of religious phenomena through depth psychology. Since depth psychology has an important contribution to make to our work, the limits of this particular discipline must be very clearly defined. This is all the more necessary because the definition of religious ideas through depth psychology is still under the influence of a psychologistic mode of thinking which limits religious phenomena and thus falsifies them. The important thing is that an inseparable connection with a reality completely transcending the internal and external world is inherent in religious phenomena as such. If, then, we apply the so-called *amplification* method[9] developed by Jung – the comparison of symbols which enriches the understanding of them – we can see the archetypes, to which they go back, in a *cosmological* and not merely in a limited psychological light. The same applies to all our borrowings from depth psychology.

The phenomenology of religion is also distinct from the sociology of religion, in that the latter is concerned exclusively with the social function of religion. Although the tradition of the Satan cult and the black mass is extremely interesting from a sociological point of view, we can consider this side of our subject only as a secondary theme. It is to be hoped that a more thorough study of the Satan cult from the sociological side will one day be made.

PART ONE

The Origins

Essential though it is to consider the question of the origins of Satan worship, it would be idle to pretend that we can find a common basis for all the phenomena described in this book. The following pages are an attempt not to deduce the nature of Satan worship from given circumstances, but to show the conditions necessary for its emergence. Only the persistent combination of these conditions with spontaneous and irrational factors could produce the phenomena which are the object of our study.

1 THE RELIGIOUS AND CULTURAL BASIS OF SATAN WORSHIP

Before the Hellenistic period, classical antiquity knew no figures comparable with Satan. The religions of the old European civilisations contained dark powers of various kinds, but they are not cast off or excluded from the divine cosmos; they are an inseparable part of it.

The Minotaur. *(Greek coin)*

The centre of the cult of Minoan Crete was the Great Goddess, whose connection with the underworld is expressed both by the fact that she was worshipped in caverns in the earth and by her attribute, the snake. The Cretan world has, on the whole, an earthy, Dionysian character; in fact it may be, as Karl Kerenji believes,[1] the birthplace of the cult of Dionysus. The legend of the Minotaur, which took shape in Grecian times, also bears witness to the integration of the infernal with the divine. But the Minotaur, known in mythology as 'Asterios' ('star'), a name of Dionysus, must be considered as one of the forms in which this god appears.[2]

It has been common knowledge since Nietzsche's *Geburt der Tragödie aus dem Geiste der Musik* (1872) that the polarity of Apollo, light, and Dionysus, darkness, was an essential feature of the Greek religion. (We know now, however, that in equating the Dionysian element with religious ecstasy Nietzsche set too narrow limits on it; it embraces also the whole of vegetative nature.[3] Dionysus and his followers represent the depths which are related in every way to the radiant spheres of the Olympian divinities. 'The Greek religion reached its most lofty heights in the link between Dionysus and Apollo . . . Apollo with Dionysus, the drunken leader of the earthly dance, is the whole measure of the world' (Walter F. Otto).[4]

Hecate. *(Roman talisman)*

There are many examples in the Greek religion of the combination of darkness and light to form a perfect whole. The earthy Titans appear both as the ancestors of the Olympians and as their bitter enemies. The python, after being conquered by Apollo, becomes the guardian of the world's centre at Delphi. Hermes, the guide of souls and the messenger of the gods, is at the same time a rogue, and often a cruel one.[5] Nature in all its wildness is embodied in his son Pan, the 'goat-footed, double-horned lover of riotous orgies, who wanders through tree-studded pastures with gaily dancing nymphs'.[6] Hecate, whose three faces show her to be a moon-goddess, is not only the mother of ghosts, a terrifying figure surrounded by whining dogs, coming to haunt travellers at crossroads; she also helps sailors and hunters, those seeking justice and women in childbed.

The same applies to the religion of Rome before the Hellenistic period. It was not until this period, when the old gods had lost their original power, that the picture changed. 'As the Eastern religions and their conceptions flowed into the Western world, all kinds of demonism came with them. . . . Besides Egyptian and Chaldean influences, a particularly important part was played by an idea stemming from dualism: the figure of the Devil and his host of evil spirits, fed on the flesh and the smoke of sacrifices, that enter into the bodies of men, causing disease and evils of every kind.[7] So, what we have called the perfect whole, formed of darkness and light, was finally broken. This influenced also the Roman *Bacchanalia* and *Saturnalia*[8] in the sense of a certain degeneration. From this Saturnus got his bad and 'diabolical' aspect.

This Persian dualism, which influenced Western thought, bringing unforeseeable consequences, can be characterised by a quotation from the Avesta, which expresses the absolute opposition between good (embodied in Ahura Mazdāh) and evil (embodied in Angra-mainyu): 'And I will speak of the two spirits at the very beginning of life, the Holy One of which said to the Evil One: Our thoughts, our teachings, our knowledge and belief, our words, deeds, consciences and souls, will never agree.'[9]

This dualism became one of the main sources of the Gnosticism, the origin of which must be sought in pre-Christian times.[10] The basic conception of dualism was common to all the various trends of gnosticism, and it also formed the basis for the gnostic doctrine of redemption.

In Christianity the ancient Hellenistic tradition was fused with the Jewish heritage, the substance of which is to be found in the Old Testament. In this tradition also, the original combination of light and darkness in one divinity was subjected to a process of evolution tending towards dualism.

Rivkah Schärf, in her important work *Die Gestalt des Satans im*

Alten Testament,[11] has made it clear by means of a large number of single interpretations that the figure of Satan emerged only in the course of the development of the Old Testament, which should be seen in the context of the history of Near-Eastern religions. The process led from the *mal'āk Jahure*, the angel in the story of Balaam (Num. 22: 22ff), which embodies the dark side of the ambivalent deity, through Satan as one of the *benē hā'elōhīm*, the sons of God, in the Book of Job (1: 6ff and 2: 1ff) to the development of Satan as the opponent of the *mal'āk Jahure* (Zach. 3: 1ff) and the independent demon (1 Chr. 21: 1). 'The separation of Satan from God, by which he was 'cleansed' of his darkness, had immense consequences. It was the starting-point for the New Testament development of Satan as the antagonist of God, and for his complete separation as expressed in the legend of the imprisoned Beast of the Apocalypse.[12]

Another part of Christianity's heritage from Judaism is the late Jewish apocalyptic tradition. In later New Testament times the Church took over from it the conception of Antichrist, the origin of which can be traced back to before the Exile. The Antichrist embodies the final aspect of Satan.[13]

In addition to the events in religious history among which Christianity took shape, we must also take into account the cultural history of the late Roman period. Rome had at this time a markedly decadent culture, in which destructive licentiousness – coarse and over refined at the same time – dominated, leading to a general disintegration of morals. A counterbalance, like that of the mystery-religion of the Indo-Persian god of light, Mithrus,[14] had become urgently necessary.

This was the beginning of the vigorous opposition of the young Church. It turned into demons the dark powers whose cult had become a part of the general decadence, and made severe moral demands on its followers. Based on the dualistic doctrines of the Jewish religion in its later stages, and influenced by the Hellenistic belief in demons and by gnostic dualism – the Church did not only fight gnosticism, but was influenced by it in many ways[15] – it opposed the 'Apollonian' principle to the 'Dionysian'; the God of goodness and light, become man in Christ, to the infernal powers of darkness and evil with Satan at their head. Early Christianity proclaimed itself with fire and passion. Two texts may serve to illustrate this. Clement of Alexandria, who died before AD 215, contrasts the Dionysian with the Christian mysteries in his *Logos protreptikos*.

Come, O madman, cease your leaning on the leafy staff of the vine, and your crowning with ivy. Take off the garland from your brow, take off the deerskin, and put on wisdom. I will show you the *Word*, and the mysteries of the *Word*. . . . There you see the mountain beloved of God, not like Cithaeron the subject of tragedies, but the mountain that rises high into the clouds and is shaded by the forests of chastity. The unholy Maenads, sisters of Semele, the lightning-stricken goddess, vowed to the tearing of living flesh, do not dance upon it in a drunken ecstasy. Here dance the daughters of God, the fair lambs, proclaiming the festival of the *Word*, raising their wise and sober chorus. The choir is the choir of the righteous, the song is a hymn to God Omnipotent. There virgins sing, angels glorify, prophets speak; the echo resounds in the far distance, and they run and follow the holy band. They are called and run with eagerness to embrace the Father. Come, you too, old man. Leave Thebes and your art of prophecy; fling aside the robes of Bacchus and let yourself be led to the truth. I will give you the Cross as a staff. Hurry, Tiresias! Believe, and you shall see. Christ shines, he shines more brightly than the sun, so that the blind can see. Night flees from you, fire is afraid, death departs. Old man, you shall see heaven as you never saw Thebes. Oh, true sacred mysteries! O clear, pure light! Led by torches, I see God and Heaven within my view. Whilst I am initiated, I become holy. The Lord is herald of the Mysteries; he gives light to the initiate and puts the seal on his brow, and presents the believer to the Father to keep for eternity. That is the Bacchic feast of my Mysteries. If you are resolved, dedicate yourself also, and join the angels in singing around the immortal, unbegotten, only true God, the Word of God, raising the hymn with us.[16]

The second text, a passage from the first *Mystagogic catechesis* of Cyril of Jerusalem dating from the year AD 348, refers to the renunciation of Satan as part of the rite of baptism:

First you go into the anteroom of the baptistery. Having taken up your position facing west, you begin to listen. Then you are commanded to stretch out your hand, and you denounce Satan as though he were present. . . . As the West is the region of visible darkness, and Satan is darkness and rules in darkness, you look towards the West, as a symbolic gesture, when you denounce that dark lord. What, now, standing, has each of you said? 'I renounce thee, Satan. I renounce thee, evil and most cruel tyrant . . . I renounce thee, sly and cunning serpent . . . I renounce thee, Satan, the author and servant of all evil. . . . A second formula requires you to say 'and all thy works'. All sins belong to the works of Satan. You renounce . . . all unreasonable deeds and thoughts. . . . Further, you say 'and all his pomps and vanities'. But the pomps of the devil include the theatre, horse-racing, hunting, and all such vanities. . . . And everything that is hung in heathen temples, or in markets on heathen festivals, whether meat or bread or the like, belongs to the pomps of the devil, because it is besmirched by the invocation of foul demons. . . . Hereupon you say 'and thy service'. The service of the Devil is to pray in heathen temples, to honour lifeless idols, to light lamps and burn incense to springs or rivers. . . . If, now, you renounce Satan and all his pack, and completely sever the old ties that bind you to Hell, then God's paradise, which he planted in the East, but from which our first father was driven out for his sins, will be opened to you. As a token of this you turn from the West to the East, the region of light. . . .[17]

In the following centuries a systematic demonology took shape;[18] we can only give an outline of it here. Originally there were only good angels. Sometime before the creation of the world a number of them, led by Lucifer ('light-bearer') rebelled against God. This sin on the part of the angels is interpreted by theologians in various ways: many see in it the refusal to acknowledge the manhood of Christ – proclaimed beforehand to the angels – and the consequent exaltation of the Virgin Mary, because it implied subjection to human nature. Others speak of Lucifer's arrogant demand to be equal to God, and thus a partner in the hypostatic union with God. Yet others say that Lucifer demanded to exercise his dominion independently of God and to be worshipped by the other angels. The rebellion was followed by the fall of the angels, in which Lucifer and his followers, on God's command, were flung into the abyss of Hell by the Archangel Michael or his warriors. Satan (the name given to the fallen Lucifer) and the evil spirits have from now on their part to play in the constitution of Hell. Augustine says: 'As an artist, a great artist, God makes use even of the Devil in his service. If he could not make use of him, he would not have permitted him to exist.'[19] Satan in the form of a serpent led the first man to sin (Gen. 3: 1ff), by which the Divine Redemption became necessary and thus at last possible, as various theologians have concluded. The influence of Satan and the other devils upon mankind has been described in detail by the demonologists, subjected to tests of many kinds, and used to form conclusions for or against God. Finally the powers of Satan as Antichrist (1 John 2: 18) will be massed together once more. The Apocalypse shows, in grandiose images, how the powers of Antichrist are concentrated before their defeat, in the fiery Dragon from heaven (12: 1ff), the Beast from the sea worshipped by sinful Man (13: 1ff), the Beast from the earth (13: 11ff) and the whore of Babylon (17: 1ff). At the Last Judgement (Rev. 20: 11ff) Satan and his evil spirits, with the damned souls, are finally separated from the good and delivered over for eternity to the torments of Hell. The new Heaven and new Earth which are then established (Rev. 21: 1ff), will be entirely free from Satan's influence.

The dogmatic conceptions of Satan and the evil spirits were in the course of time enriched and varied by folk elements of many kinds, arising partly from the mythological traditions of different races (the Germanic, for example). We shall speak of this aspect, which is particularly important for the understanding of the Satan cult, at the appropriate point in our study.

In the Christian religion the defeat of Satan's power plays an essential part from the very beginning, starting with the *abrenuntiatio*, the renunciation of Satan in the baptism service, which remains to this day (see above). Not only exorcism in its narrow sense, but many other ritual acts were intended to ward off demons. The same applies to many Christian folk customs.

With these facts in mind, what significance are we to give to Satan worship and the black mass? Five points are to be considered:

1 The cult of Satan developed on the basis of the dualistic conception of Christianity. The realms of thought which Christianity as a whole rejected and proscribed for the reasons given, made a direct though distorted appearance in Satanism.

2 The cult of Satan constitutes a collective protest movement, for which we shall not here give further evidence, psychological or otherwise. That is to say it is the extreme antithesis of Christianity and has therefore one-sided and exaggerated features which are the cause of its distorted and usually destructive character.

3 As well as this negative and antithetic function, the Satan cult has a compensating function with respect to the tradition of the Christian Church. This has been particularly so since the historical circumstances in which Christianity took shape have substantially altered.

4 The cult of Satan is thus completely ambivalent; it is destructive and creative at the same time. By attacking the established order at its roots it produces an impression of one-sidedness on a vast scale; and, equally, by clearly differentiating, it gives us a perfect picture of the whole.

5 The two religions, Christianity and Satanism, are inseparable one from the other. They are the two poles that mark the field of tension that determines our civilisation and its destiny.

The Preaching of Anti-Christ. *(Woodcut, 15th cent.)*

2 SOCIOLOGICAL ASPECTS OF SATANIC MOVEMENTS

The points just listed include some sociological points of view. If we look closely at the tradition of Satan worship it is clear how important social conditions are, even in small details, for the origin and structure of the phenomenon. However, as we said in the Introduction, we can consider this side only as secondary, and must stop at a few general indications.

Bo Reicke,[1] in the work *Diakonie, Festfreude und Zelos in Verbindung mit der altchristliche Agapefeier*, shows that the signs of decadence in the 'love-feasts', constantly subjected to severe criticism in the New Testament, were closely connected with political and social trends of the time, being a part of the revolutionary anti-Roman movements, both Jewish and heathen. The same applies to many societies for the worship of Satan; they brought together men who felt frustrated by the contemporary order of society and had therefore fallen into a state of more or less serious social disintegration. The practices of the Satanist communities which originated in this way, and which regularly formed new standards of behaviour within the group, allowed both the expression of protest and a compensatory fulfilment of expectations disappointed by an institutionalised culture. The fanaticism of the Satanists and their persecutors bears out the observation that conflicts between groups are fiercer the nearer the warring groups are to each other.[2] The cult of Satan is a direct perversion by apostates of the ritual of the Church.

The Satan cult can be considered from various points of view, involving both group sociology and sometimes even mass sociology (the latter applies especially to the witches' sabbath of the late Middle Ages).[3] We shall confine ourselves to brief incidental notes on this subject as the occasion arises.

Alfred Weber says in his work *Kulturgeschichte als Kultursoziologie* that he does not believe that 'it is really possible to provoke collective activity unless the immediate picture of life and humanity called up by each person originates, perhaps unconsciously, on a higher plane. It is only on this level that we can gain the experience necessary to release the spiritual force we need.'[4] The area to which these words refer falls within the scope of religious phenomenology, but not of sociology. We must therefore concentrate our attention on this 'higher plane' as it appears in the cult of Satan.

3 THE PSYCHOPATHOLOGICAL FEATURES OF SATAN WORSHIP

Psychopathy, in the narrow sense of the word, means 'mental deviations of a congenital nature, of long duration, which do not follow a course of development, but remain stationary'.[1] It is thus differentiated on the one hand from the progressive psychoses and on the other hand from the neuroses which are acquired mental illnesses. However, in what follows we are using the word 'psychopathic' in a wide sense, meaning 'mentally sick' in general.

We can see from a superficial glance at the forms in which the Satan cult appears that the initiators of such rites and those who take part in them must in very many cases be regarded as either psychopathic or in extreme danger of becoming so. Nevertheless, as we have already stressed in the Introduction, it is not enough to postulate an entirely psychopathic basis for the Satan cult. This chapter, therefore, deals only with a very limited aspect of the subject.

First of all we should say that mental abnormality provides particularly favourable conditions for extreme modes of behaviour to take place – a fact which applies to a relatively high number of saints and their imitators, though with opposite consequences. The Satan cult thus offers its adherents the possibility of fulfilling urges which are abnormal, that is to say prohibited by normal society; this is an essential reason for its appeal to the mentally sick.

If we are to make a more detailed analysis of the Satan cult from a psychopathological point of view, we must differentiate between male and female psychology.

With regard to male psychology, Sigmund Freud (whom we are following here only in his psychoanalytical explanation, not in his psychologistic interpretation of his findings) in his work *Eine Teufelsneurose im ziebzehnten Jahrhundert*, published in 1923, showed that the figure of the Devil was a projection of the negative side of the father-figure. The importance of this point of view merits a somewhat longer quotation:

We do not need much analytical perspicacity to divine that God

> and the Devil were originally identical, one single figure which was later divided into two with opposite characteristics.[3] In the earliest days of religion God himself still possessed all the terrifying features which were subsequently combined in his antagonist. It is the well-known process of the splitting of an idea that is ambivalent in content into two sharply contrasting opposites. But the contradictions in the original nature of God are a reflection of the individual's ambivalent attitude to his own father. If the good and just God is a father-substitute, it is not surprising that the hostile attitude of hate and fear and resentment should also be expressed, in the figure of Satan. The father is thus the individual prototype of both God and the devil.[4]

And Freud says in a note: 'If we dare to affirm that the devil, historically, is a father-substitute, we can see the mediaeval witch-trials in a new light.'[5] It is obvious that Christian Devil-hatred, in its male, inquisitorial sense, can easily be interpreted on this basis. But what connection has this with antichristian Devil-worship?

To understand the latter, we must assume the existence of two so-called 'defence mechanisms'.[6] The first has been called 'reactive alteration' in psychoanalysis. This means in our case that the oedipal hate against the negative, castrating side of the father-image, represented by Satan, is transformed into love with the help of overcompensation or 'reaction-formation' in the form of the reinforcing effect of ritual. At the same time the negative aspect of the father-image itself is transformed to its opposite, and the hostile castrating father becomes the universal source of strength. But here a second defence mechanism comes into play: 'identification with the aggressor'. This means the introjection of the object of fear, which helps the transformation of fear to security. In a remarkable analogy with the Christians' participation in the Body of Christ, the Satanists identify themselves with the Satan-figure and its negative tendencies, giving rise to their aggressive behaviour towards Christian society. By means of this 'diversion' of the negative tendency the sphere of conflict is shifted, and becomes external rather than internal.[7] Once the inner world of the psyche is made secure by the defence mechanism, the separation from the negative father-image takes place in the external world, that is to say in the struggle against the symbols of traditional Christianity.

If we look at the Satan cult from the point of view of female psychology, the picture changes. Here too Satan represents a side of the father-image; not the negative side, however, but the one that gratifies the incompletely repressed impulses of early childhood. When we see how decisive a part sexual union with the Devil (or his representative) plays in women's worship of Satan, we have to allow that the Devil, for his female adherents, becomes by projection the oedipal love-object, once utterly unattainable, and now at last within their grasp. (Here too there are parallels in the Christian tradition; we have only to think of the religious ecstasies of female mystics, often sexually coloured.) Again a defence mechanism comes into play; but in women the hate-impulse is directed against the mother, and, by a process of transference, against the Christian world. Here too the conflict becomes external rather than internal.

For reasons to be explained later, women dominate both quantitatively and qualitatively in circles practising Satan worship (for example, as 'Queen of the Sabbath'). They enable men to project the object of their oedipal desire – that is to say the mother-image – and thus to satisfy their libidinal urges. The medieval witches exercised a great fascination even over their persecutors, and this, by the mechanism of 'reaction-formation' which we have mentioned, became bitter hatred and a passionate will to exterminate.

The Satan cult as a whole, viewed psychopathologically, is a large-scale regression in the psychoanalytical sense – a return to early infantile phases of emotional development. The figure of Satan serves not only as a father-image in the narrow sense but also as a paternal authority which allows this regression and thus prevents guilt-feelings – in fact a protective super-ego within the psyche. Besides the regressive fulfilment of incestuous urges (sometimes even in a directly familiar form) and the corresponding aggressive impulses, the cult of Satan offers its participants a particularly far-reaching opportunity to regress to the so-called anal-sadistic stage of emotional development. It is not surprising that it acts as a reservoir for psychopathic individuals of many types.

It has not been possible to give more than a sketchy outline of the psychopathology of the Satan cult. We shall come back to some of it later, but our study is concerned mainly with other fields, which must be explored if the psychopathological data are to be placed in their proper context.

PART TWO

Documents Relating to the Satan Cult and the Black Mass

4 FRINGE MANIFESTATIONS OF THE SATAN CULT IN THE FIRST CENTURIES OF THE CHRISTIAN ERA

A *Gnostic cults: the communion of the Phibionites and the Ophites*

1 The Phibionites belong to a group of Gnostic sects to which Hans Leisegang gives the collective name of 'Barbelo-gnosticism'[1] because their doctrine is centred on the figure of 'Barbelo' (or 'Barbero'). Barbelo – opinions differ on the derivation of the name[2] – is the 'Great Mother' present in the divine fullness of spiritual existence, the Pleroma of the Father. She is thus an incarnation of the Asiatic-Egyptian mother-divinity. Her antagonist is her son, the 'Archon of this world', the evil creator, who has succeeded through his creatures in robbing his mother of her divine powers and dispersing them about the world. The mission of the Gnostics is to snatch these powers from the Archon and bring them back to the Upper Heaven and thus to the Great Mother. The cult is dedicated to this work of redemption.

The fellowship of Phibionites was founded in Syria (where they were called Koddians), and spread to Armenia and Egypt. Around the year AD 200, groups of Phibionites infiltrated the Christian Church, and the fusion of their original rites with the Christian Eucharist gave rise to the Phibionite Communion.[3]

About the year 335 a doctor of the Church, Epiphanius of Salamis in Egypt, who was then about twenty years old, came into close contact with the Phibionites. He studied their writings and their cult, and was almost persuaded to join the sect, whose members belonged to the Christian communities. However, after a time Epiphanius left the Phibionites, and when they mocked him he denounced them to the ecclesiastical authorities, whereupon the eighty members of the sect were expelled from the Church. The following account by Epiphanius can therefore be considered as coming from an eyewitness:

Epiphanius, Panarion haer. XXVI, 4, 5. Ed. Holl., I, p. 280ff (Migne PG 357ff) *

They have their women in common. And in case there is anyone

* References to source documents are given in full in the appendix.

present who is a stranger to their doctrines, there is a signal given by the men to the women and by the women to the men in the manner in which they shake hands in greeting; they touch the palm with a kind of tickling movement, and by this they know whether the stranger is a member of their community. When they have thus recognised each other they immediately begin their feast. They serve rich foods, eat meat and drink wine even if they are poor. When they have eaten together, and, to speak figuratively, strength has flowed into their veins, they fall into a frenzy. And the man moves away from his wife, and tells his own wife to go and make the Agape with his brother. And these wretches copulate with each other, and though I am truly ashamed to relate their foul actions (in the words of the holy apostle, what happens among them is 'shameful even to mention'[a]) yet I will not shame to say what they do not shame to do, and I shall make all who hear me shudder at their disgusting practices. For after they have copulated, not content with the sin of fornication, they increase still more their own blasphemy against Heaven; both man and woman take in their own hands that which flowed from the man, stand up and turn towards Heaven with the filth on their hands, and utter the prayer of so-called Stratiotiki and Gnostics, in which they offer the stuff on their hands to the Father of All, with the words: 'We bring thee this gift, the body of Christ.' And then they eat it, making a communion of their shame, and say: 'This is the body of Christ, and this is the Passover through which our bodies will suffer and be forced to recognise the suffering of Christ.' They do the same with whatever comes from the woman, even if it is in the form of a flow of blood, taking the menstrual blood that comes from her unclean condition. And they say: 'This is the blood of Christ.' And when they read in the Apocalypse 'I saw a tree bearing fruit twelve times in a year, and he said to me: this is the Tree of Life',[b] they give it the allegorical meaning of the woman's monthly flow of blood.

But if they have intercourse with each other, it is not with the idea of begetting children. For this wickedness is not perpetrated by them to beget children, but for pleasure, since the Devil is playing tricks on them and mocking the image of God. But they

[a] Eph. 5: 12
[b] Rev. 22: 2

take their pleasure to its conclusion, and then instead of letting the seed of their fornication penetrate far enough to produce children, they take it for themselves, and eat the fruit of their shame. But if one of them is careless enough to let his seed gush forth so that it penetrates deeply, and the woman becomes pregnant, then hear what greater evil they dare do. They rip out the embryo at the moment when it can be held in the hands, and take this foetus and crush it in a kind of mortar with a pestle, and mix with it honey and pepper and certain other herbs and fragrant oils, so that it may not disgust them: and then all this community of pigs and dogs assembles, and each communicates, taking some of the murdered child with his fingers. And when they have finished this cannibal feast, they finally pray to God, saying: 'We were not letting ourselves be tricked by the Archon of lust, but were collecting together the transgressions of our brother.' And this, forsooth, they consider the perfect communion.

And they perpetrate many other such horrors. If they fall once again into such frenzy, they smear their hands with their disgusting sperm, stretch them out, and pray with their hands besmirched and their whole body naked, as though by this action they could achieve free speech with God. Both men and women tend their bodies night and day with ointments, baths and diet, and they spend their time in sleep and drinking. And they curse those who fast, saying they should not fast, for fasting belongs to that Archon who created the Aeon. Rather they should nourish themselves, so that their bodies may be strong and bring forth fruit in their time.

We find signals like the one described at the beginning of the text in many secret societies, including the early Christians at the time of the persecution. Considering the character of their cult, the fact that the Phibionites tickled the inside of each others' hands on greeting suggests a partly erotic significance.[4]

The ritual begins with the feast and the 'Agape'. The feast is expressly described as rich, and the Agape consists of the sexual union of the participants. This provides a glaring contrast to the attitude of the old church, which is expressed in concentrated form in the passage from the Epistle to the Romans – which has become famous in connection with the conversion of St Augustine – in which St Paul exhorts the Romans to indulge in 'no revelling or drunkenness, no debauchery or vice' but to 'throw off the deeds of darkness' (13: 12 and 13). But we should miss the sense of the phenomenon if we left it at that. The feast and the sexual union are here *res sacrae* – sacred actions.

Eating and drinking together corresponds to the early Christian love-feast (this introduced the celebration of the Eucharist until the end of the second century, and did not become a separate ritual until then) and to many similar customs in a variety of religious traditions. Its purpose is to bind together the members of the cult and make of them true participants in the mystery.

The richness of the meal has a clearly anti-spiritual significance; whereas the Christian Church limits as far as possible the material side of the substances used in the cult, together with the ceremonies involved, and lays the emphasis on the spiritual and invisible effect (a fact which we shall discuss in more detail later), in this case the material side is of extreme importance. But one essential point is to be noted here. The Gnostics have the task of liberating as many as possible of the forces imprisoned by the Archon in creation – that is, in plants and animals as well as in man – and to assemble them in order to bring them back to the 'world-soul' – in this case Barbelo. This liberation and assembling is accomplished in the act of eating. The richness of the feast thus ensures that as many forces as possible can be captured and returned to their celestial source.

As far as the anti-spiritual character is concerned, this is even more obvious in the accomplishment of the Agape. The Church uses the Greek word *agape* to mean spiritual love in opposition to sensual love. But in this case 'to make the Agape' exactly corresponds to the French expression *faire l'amour*, that is to say the word 'Agape' is understood in an entirely concrete and physical way. The basic spiritual tradition of Christianity recognises the sexual act as a religious symbol only within a legitimate marriage; but for the Phibionites the act as such, in common with the Hierosgamos (sacred marriage) rites of many races, has a religious and symbolic function. Their promiscuity ('they have their women in common') emphasises, as is often the case with similar customs, the fact that the sexual rite goes beyond the personal aspect. From the Christian point of view, of course, this appears as a mere quest for *hēdonē*, pleasure, which Epiphanius attributes to the work of the Devil, an interpretation which specifically justifies the treatment of the Phibionites' feast as a marginal phenomenon of Satan worship.

According to the doctrine of the Phibionites, the sexual act must not lead to the begetting of children; instead, the sperm is collected to be used in the rite which follows. Here the contrast with Christian teaching is an extreme one; in the opinion of the theologians the procreation of children is one of the most important aims – according to some even the first aim (*finis primarius*) – of sexual union, so that Catholic moral theology strictly forbids any mechanical means to prevent this result. Many medieval theologians even went so far as to say that demons were conceived from seed that had not been put to its natural use.

In order to understand why the Phibionites were urged to avoid having children, we must realise that it is a basic part of gnostic belief to view the seed as good in itself, charged with divine power; but the begetting of new human beings is to be prevented in order to keep the domain of the Archon who rules creation as small as possible. The Archon is thus to be tricked through the sexual act.

Now follows the offering of the sperm, described here by Epiphanius as 'filth'. The Phibionites raised to heaven their sperm-covered hands – according to the last paragraph of our text they do this naked – addressing these words to God the Father: 'We offer thee this gift, the body of Christ.' It is an exact parallel with the Church's sacrificial offering, the 'Anaphora'. In order to clarify the meaning of this action, we must first look more closely at the symbolism of the sperm for the Gnostics.

Sperm has been regarded since very ancient times as endowed with mysterious power or *mana*,[5] and so has a part to play in many magical rites and in the folklore of antiquity.[6] On a higher level it is directly associated with the *pneuma*, the life-giving breath of the Spirit, a connection which emerges particularly clearly in Democrites, Aristotle and the Stoics.[7] In the Septuagint the Hebrew word *rūah* for the spirit of God that hovered over the face of the waters at the beginning of Creation is translated *pneuma*. This was the origin of the Gnostics' speculations. It was believed 'that this pneuma is nothing more or less than sperm, the life-giving stuff that created the world and mankind. The pneuma is thus the Godhead itself, possessed by man in his own seed . . . To be united with God means that one's seed is fused into one with the seed of the universe. To be redeemed means to release one's seed from its earthly destiny and return it to the divine source of all seed.'[8]

In the Phibionites' feast, the sperm, corresponding to the bread in the liturgy of the Church, becomes the body of Christ; this rests upon two premises. It is a return to the early Christian, pre-Nicene belief according to which Christ and the Holy Ghost, the Logos and the Pneuma, were almost the same thing,[9] and at the same time Christ, as the 'Pneuma', is identified with the divine pneuma which the Gnostics believed to be present in sperm.

The essence of the Church's communion service is the Anaphora. It is in essence a hymn, with a succession of fixed structural elements (Eucharist, Anamnesis, Epiclesis).[10] The Anaphora is based on two ideas, consecration and sacrifice. The Phibionite Anaphora is limited to the sacrifical aspect, and this is expressed in one single sentence (occurring in the old form of the liturgy usually at the end of the Anamnesis, the commemoration of Christ's work of healing). By offering the sperm to the Omnipresent Father, whose wholeness, or Pleroma, embraces the Earth mother, the might of the Archon, who stole the divine powers from Heaven, is broken. These powers, in the form of sperm, are concentrated in Christ, the 'Anti-Archon', and return to their source as a 'gift'.

Epiphanius explains the liturgical nakedness of the Phibionites as allowing a particularly free approach to God. The ritual nakedness[11] which is widespread among many races often has this meaning. In this case the sexual aspect certainly also plays a part.

The Anaphora is followed by the communion of the sperm. The act of redemption is introduced by the offering to the All-Father of the divine stuff of the spirit incarnate in the bodies of men. Its completion comes when the Gnostics, communicating with the sperm, receive back the divine powers and are only then truly redeemed. The introductory words of the communion service, in a slightly altered form, express the consecratory aspect of the ritual – not, however, in the sense of a means of bringing about the consecration, but as a demonstration that the sperm used in communion is consecrated, that is to say the Body of Christ.[12] The form of communion goes on to speak of the Passover (later called the *perfect pascha*) which, through the popular derivation of *pascha* from *paschein*,[13] is equated with the sufferings of Christ. The words obviously mean the whole ritual. The Eucharist of the Church is understood as the renewal of Christ's sacrifice on the cross and man's participation in it; and the situation is the same here, but altered in meaning to suit Gnostic doctrine. The sufferings of the Christ present in the sperm consist in his expulsion from Heaven; caused by the Archon, and his diffusion throughout creation. The Gnostic, taking in the body of Christ in the form of sperm, participates in this suffering, which will end only when Christ, who has 'flowed out' into the world, has completely returned to the divine Pleroma, and Creation, the realm of the Archon, no longer exists. Thus the feast of the Phibionites, like the Christian liturgy, takes on an eschatological aspect; it is the beginning and the anticipation of the end of the world.

As the sperm, for the Phibionites, takes the place of the eucharistic bread, so the menstrual blood takes the place of the wine. Like the sperm, the menstrual blood has been seen from the earliest times as endowed with *mana*, that is to say supernatural power. It plays a great part in magic as the bringer of either good or bad luck.[14] In antiquity it was often considered as the seed of the woman. Pliny says: '. . . this is the stuff of procreation, by which the seed of the man is fused together like a molten mass, and in time gains life and shape.'[15] We can assume that the parallel use of the menstrual blood with the sperm in the Phibionite communion rests on this idea. The divine forces are present, not only in the male but also in the female 'sperm'. But in addition the ritual use of the menstrual blood has a special meaning connected with the belief in Barbelo: the menstrual blood, with its matriarchal implications, is naturally a vehicle for the power of the Great Mother.

Horrible though the Phibionites' eating of the embryo, of which Epiphanius goes on to tell us, may be, it follows naturally according to the basic religious ideas of this sect. The danger that the Archon's realm may be increased through the birth of a new human being must be obviated, and through the communion of the foetus the divine power trapped in the creature by the Archon will be liberated and 'gathered in' for the use of the All-Mother once more. The Phibionites thus identify themselves with the negative, devouring aspect of the Eternal Feminine personified in Barbelo: 'This terrible Female is the greedy earth that eats its own children and feeds on their corpses, the vulture and the coffin, the flesh-eating tomb, whose grinning jaws greedily lick up the blood-seed of man and beast.[16] Barbelo here corresponds to the gruesome Hindu goddess Kali and the Phibionites to her servants.[17] The doctrine and cult of Christianity have accepted the bright, positive side of the primeval female element (we shall discuss this in more detail later), and the negative side has been driven back into other spheres. It is only by postulating a process of splitting that we can understand the opposition of the Holy Church and the unholy 'fellowship of pigs and dogs' as Epiphanius calls the Phibionites.

In contrast to the Church's demand for the mortification of the flesh, the Phibionites took care of their bodies and rejected fasting; this too is an anti-spiritual trait. At the same time the prohibition of fasting is also motivated by the notion of 'gathering in' divine powers through eating.

2 *Ophites* (from the Greek *ophis*, serpent) is the term used by the Fathers of the Church for a family of Gnostic sects, whose doctrine and religious rites are centred on the serpent.[18] Hippolytus knew three Ophitic communities: the Noassenes, the Perates and the Sethians. The following description, by Epiphanius, probably relates to the liturgical practice of a sect closely allied to the Perates.[19]

Epiphanius, Panarion haer. XXXVII, 3, ed. Holl., I, p. 57ff (Migne PG XLI, 648ff)

They have a serpent in its natural state, which they carry in a box, and when the time comes for their mysteries they bring it out of its hiding-place, and heaping bread on a table they call to the serpent, and when its hiding-place is opened it comes out. When the snake, in its wisdom and cunning, comes up, and at once realises their stupidity, it goes on to the table and wraps itself around the bread. And this, they say, is the perfect sacrifice. And then, as I heard from someone, they do not only break the bread in which the serpent has entwined itself and divide it among the communicants, but each also kisses the serpent with his lips, since the serpent has been tamed by means of a magic incantation, or tricked and made gentle by other devilish powers. They throw themselves down before it, and that around which the serpent has coiled they call Eucharist; and raising a hymn to the Father above through the serpent, as they say, they end their mysteries.

We must first of all study the symbolism of the serpent.[20] This will be done in rather more detail because the serpent plays an important part in everything to do with Satan and his cult.

The snake symbol at its first level is the Uroboros, the snake in the shape of a circle, biting its tail.[21] The serpent in this form represents a primitive situation, both cosmic and psychic, in which there are still no differentiated extremes. An image of eternity before any existence is the Uroboros coiled around Heaven like a ring.

At the second level of meaning the serpent embodies the dark chthonic side of nature, both human and divine. Since it thus belongs to the realms of matriarchy, the Great Earth mother is often given snakes as an attribute. From a psychological point of view the serpent symbolises instinct and impulse, or the unconscious in general. This meaning may be the starting-point for the Hindu conception of the serpent of Kundalini, which climbs upwards, that is, to consciousness, in the spinal cord. On the same level the serpent may also mean the primitive and instinctive aspect of the male element (the serpent representing the phallus).

The third level of meaning appears in dualistic religious systems. The symbol now becomes definitely ambivalent, with negative and positive aspects.

In its negative aspect the serpent, often associated with the dragon, appears as the ancient enemy of the gods of Heaven, or of divinity in general. Unlike the matriarchal civilisation of Crete, the patriarchal culture of Greece, while keeping its conception of divinity as a perfect whole compounded of darkness and light, was aware of this contrast. We need only think of the serpent-children of Gaia, or the snake-goddess Echidna, the mother of the serpent of Lerna in the story of Heracles, or the serpent of the Hesperides. It was a serpent that stole the plant of eternal youth from Gilgamesh. In the Old Testament the serpent is the tempter in Paradise, and in the shape of a dragon, Leviathan, it is the enemy of Jehovah. In Germanic mythology we can mention the serpent-like dragon, Nidhögger, that gnawed the roots of the great ash tree, Yggdrasil, and lived in enmity with the eagle high in its branches; or the Serpent of Midgard, which at the twilight of the gods uncoiled itself and unleashed the elements. In Christianity the negative symbolism of the serpent is particularly marked; here, arising from the story of the Garden of Eden, it becomes the

Abraxas. *(Gnostic talisman)*

embodiment of the power of the Devil. From the psychological point of view the serpent in this sense is the symbol of the opposition between instinct and intellect, or between the conscious and unconscious mind, giving rise to a tension that increases to an irreconcilable degree.

It is extremely interesting that the serpent had already at an early stage a completely opposite, positive aspect. It became simultaneously the bringer of knowledge, salvation and redemption. As the 'serpent of brass' placed upon a pole, it brought the Israelites healing from the bite of the fiery serpents (Num. 21:8ff); Christian symbolism saw in this a foretaste of the crucified Redeemer (John 3: 14ff). The serpent is closely connected with the god of healing, Asklepios. In later antiquity it was a symbol of the intellect. Philo of Biblos wrote, in the first century AD:

> The serpent is the most intelligent of all animals. Its nature is that of fire, and it is wonderfully swift with no need of limbs to help it. It can take on many forms, can coil itself and suddenly leap upwards. It has a long life, and from old age goes back to

> youth and gains new strength, until after a certain time has passed it is again dissolved into itself. For that reason it is used in the practice of religion and the Mysteries.[22]

Philo touches on the shape-shifting character of the serpent, connected with the annual sloughing of its skin, which causes it to become a symbol of rebirth or even immortality. In many myths and fairy tales, and in popular belief, the serpent is the guardian of hidden treasures or the bringer of the plant of eternal youth. For the alchemists the serpent is closely connected with the philosophers' stone, and in its double form it symbolises the unification of opposites. Men believed they could distil the 'highest medicine' from its venom. The positive aspect of the symbolism of the serpent is psychologically understandable if we remember that, for people of a one-sided spiritual outlook who can no longer go back to natural and instinctive sources, the serpent represents in this situation the elements of redemption, salvation and perfection. It brings not abstract knowledge but knowledge through experience (the story of the Garden of Eden); instead of effete ideas and standards it opens up the treasures of the mysterious deep, and all the abundance of the earth. In this way the serpent can become the bringer of salvation and the redeemer of the *logos*. This applies to some Hellenic mystery cults. In the Mysteries of Sabazius, for example, the serpent is the highest divinity. As a sign of unity with the Godhead, a serpent is drawn through the laps of the initiates – a rite that appears in other similar cultures.

Hans Leisegang has brought forward a very impressive testimony to Hellenic snake-worship.[23] The inside of an alabaster bowl of late antiquity shows a religious group at the highest point of its mysteries – the ascent into Heaven. The deity appears in the form of a great winged snake. The women are waiting to be received by the god, while the men assume an attitude of giving.

For the Ophites, as we have said, the serpent is a focal point; it is the *hen to pān*, all in one. The Perates see the serpent as the Logos, which has its place between God the Father, who is unchanging, and matter, which changes: 'Then it turns towards the Father and takes his power in the countenance; but when it has received the power it turns towards matter. This has no quality or form, but the Son impresses upon it the ideas which were impressed upon the Son by the Father.'[24] No one can be saved without the serpent, which is filled with the divine Pleroma. The Ophitic doctrine has innumerable variations on this idea, relating particularly to Moses' brazen serpent. All hope rests on the serpent, all power comes from it; it alone can save humanity from destruction. The whole Bible is interpreted with reference to this leitmotiv: the serpent is the river that flows out of Eden, the mark that was set on the forehead of Cain that no one might kill him; it is the 'beginning' mentioned in the first verse of St John's Gospel, and so on.[25]

On this basis our source becomes comprehensible. The Logos, embodied in the serpent, distinguished for wisdom and cunning, consecrates the host. This happens when it coils around the bread – a fact which is interesting also because some theologians, as late as the sixteenth century, assumed the validity of a *consecratio per contactum* – consecration through contact.[26] The communicant is filled with the power of the serpent, that is, the power of the redeeming Logos. Through the serpent, which is honoured with obeisances and kisses, a hymn is raised to the Father – an exact parallel to the *per Christum* (through Christ) of the Church liturgy. The use of the expression 'perfect sacrifice' may perhaps be a relic of a primitive sacrifice made to the serpent itself.[27] But in the context of the whole religious celebration it may simply mean an act of devotion to God the Father through it, that is through the serpent.

Christian tradition sees the symbol of the serpent from a predominantly negative point of view. Any aspect of the image of Christ represented by the serpent is practically not expressed at all; in fact it is attributed almost exclusively to Satan. The Ophitic serpent-image and its cult is a complete antithesis and counterbalance to the ecclesiastical *Imago Christi* and the liturgy belonging to it. The Ophite communion is thus a forerunner of the true cult of Satan.

We can deal only with the two most important fringe phenomena of the Satan cult as carried on by the Gnostics. For a more detailed picture, reference can be made to the *Dialogus de operatione Daemonum* by Michael Psellus.[28]

B *Orgiastic dances at the graves of martyrs*

In the fourth century, as Christianity became a State religion and thus a mass religion, a complex of usages with Dionysiac features began to form: the ecstatic and orgiastic dances at the graves of the martyrs. From the many available sources we have chosen two:

Basilius, Homilia XIV in ebriosos, I.
Migne PG XXXI, 445f.

Shameless women, forgetting the fear of God and scorning the eternal fire, on the very day when in memory of the Resurrection they should have stayed at home and thought of the day when the Heavens shall open and the Judge appear, the trumpets of God shall sound and the dead rise, when true judgement shall be given and everyone requited according to his deserts – such women, instead of busying themselves with such thoughts and cleansing their hearts of evil desires, washing away with tears their former sins and preparing themselves to meet Christ on the great day of his coming, have shaken off the yoke of service to Christ, and torn the veil of modesty from their heads. Holding God and his angels in contempt, they have exposed themselves shamelessly to the eyes of men. Tossing their hair and trailing their dresses, tripping with their feet, with lustful glances and unbridled laughter, they have flung themselves madly into the dance. They have attracted to themselves the young men's wantonness and danced before the town at the graves of the martyrs, turning the holy places into a stage to display their shamelessness. They have desecrated the air with their lecherous songs and desecrated with their impure feet the earth that trampled in their dances. They have gathered together a swarm of young men to watch them, whores that they are, and mad – greater madness were not possible. Could I be silent about all this? How can I berate it as it deserves? Wine has robbed us of our souls – wine, that was given by God to the temperate to restore them in sickness, but is now being used by the intemperate to help them to the most shameful of excesses.

Augustinus, Sermo CCXI, 5.
Migne XXXVIII 14/15

Once, not many years ago, the dancers invaded this place [the grave of the martyr Cyprian] with their impudence. This place, so holy, where the body of so holy a martyr lies, as many older people remember, this holy place, I say, was invaded by the dancers' pestilent impudence. All night they sang these impious songs, and as they sang, they danced. When the Lord willed it, through our holy brother your bishop, on whose order the holy vigils began to be kept here, that pestilence struggled for a little, and then yielded to diligence and blushed before wisdom.

These customs are attested in a large number of countries, both eastern and western. From the point of view of religious history they represent a process of paganisation by taking over the ancient customs of funeral feasts and funeral dances in Christian lands.[29] To understand this phenomenologically, we must go back a little.

As we have already said, the Church, in protest against the decadent culture of late classical times, maintained an attitude of firm opposition to the Dionysian rites; accordingly, it proscribed dance, which had by that time become extremely decadent and obscene. Several synods listed the profession of dancer as one of those forbidden to Christians, and the Fathers of the Church never tired of preaching against dance. John Chrysostom says in a sermon on the popular subject of Salome's dance: 'The Devil helped her to please Herod with her dance and so to capture him. For wherever there is a dance, the Devil too is there. God did not give us our feet for dancing, but for walking in the right paths; not for licentiousness, for leaping like camels (for they too, and not only women, execute repulsive dances) but for moving with the angels in the heavenly procession.'[30]

It is important to realise, however, that the Dionysian element was not completely eradicated from early Christianity; it developed in a limited and altered form on a different level. It included the early Christian prophecies, the Gift of Tongues, and most particularly the fact that in the first centuries of the Christian era the text of the liturgy was laid down only in outline, and the priest improvised freely and ecstatically. The same thing occurred with singing.[31] The words of Clement of Alexandria on p. 11 are full of this spirit.

But from the third century onwards first the words of the liturgy, then the music, gradually became fixed. The ecstatic element faded out of the Christian religion, and text and singing became frozen fossilised. The result was that the religious ceremony became markedly repetitive.

When, in the fourth century, Christianity became a popular religion, it was no longer possible completely to maintain the ban on the Dionysian element. There were no longer any Christian forms into which the Dionysian impulses could be channelled and sublimated, so these impulses had to emerge in pagan form. Even though liturgical festivals were substituted for the orgiastic dances, and some bishops even tolerated the dances themselves, the basic problem was not eliminated. A revival of the early Christian enthusiasm, which alone could have provided a solution, was not possible in a mass religion. So a lasting thorn was planted. From the wild women at the graves of the martyrs a direct line – though several centuries long – led to the wild witches of the Middle Ages.

5 THE MEDIEVAL GOLDEN AGE OF SATAN WORSHIP

It was not until the Middle Ages that the organisation of the Christian religion provided a basis upon which the Satan cult proper could take shape and develop. The flowering of the Christian mysteries in the early and high Middle Ages had its counterpart – with a chronological shift, the reasons for which will be given later – in the flowering of the Satan cult in the late Middle Ages. First of all, however, we have still some fringe phenomena to discuss.

A *Fringe phenomena: dancing mania, asses' and fools' festivals*

1 Cases of spontaneous dancing mania[1] occurred as early as the seventh and eighth centuries, but it was not until the eleventh and twelfth that it became a large-scale epidemic. This mass psychosis reached its height in the second half of the fourteenth century. More limited outbreaks of collective dancing are recorded as late as the seventeenth century.

In the eleventh and twelfth centuries dancing mania broke out most particularly in churchyards. After a death, or on Church festivals, we are told, men and women in the cemeteries surrounding the churches were suddenly seized with an irresistible compulsion to dance and sing profane songs. This usually happened at the time of Church services. The disturbers of the peace were usually cursed by the priests so that they would go on dancing without a stop. According to some stories they had to dance for a year, or until a bishop took off the curse.[2] Later on the dancing mania broke out mainly as a result of the dances on the feast of St John the Baptist, which were pagan in origin, but which Christian sources explained as being in memory of the dance of Herodias. The 'St John's dances' spread very quickly. The name 'St Vitus's Dance', by which they were later known, is probably a substitution, for the name of the Slav sun god Svantovit, of that of St Vitus ('sante Vit'), an early Christian martyr whose feast was celebrated on 15 June, very near to that of St John. The change of name was all the more likely because at one time the sun god was honoured with dances at that season.[3] A parallel phenomenon,

Tarantism, appeared in southern Italy. This was a wild dance, originally intended as a spell against the poisonous bite of the Apulian spider *Lycosa tarantula*; but then it became a mass ecstatic manifestation, from which the folk dance called the Tarentella later developed. Both Church and secular authorities tried to deal with the dancing mania by every available method – strict prohibition, exorcism, isolation of afflicted persons, the use of blows and cold water, and even intensification of the dance in order to exhaust the dancers. All these measures met at best with very slight success.

The following source describes the beginning of the great wave of dancing mania that started in the Rhine and Moselle districts in the year 1374.

From the Limburger Chronik, ed. Vogel, p. 71

In the year 1374, in the middle of summer, a strange thing happened on earth, and in particular in the land of Germany, on the Rhine and on the Moselle. People began to dance and to act wildly, and they took up positions, one couple facing another, and they danced on the same spot for half a day, and while dancing they often fell down and let people step on their bodies. They claimed that they had thus achieved salvation. And they ran from one town to another, and from one church to another, and got money from people as they could. And it got to such a pitch that more than five hundred dancers were found in the city of Cologne. And it was found that it was a heresy, and that it was done for money, and some of them, men and women, fell into and committed fornication. And there in Cologne more than a hundred women and serving-maids were found who had no husbands. All of these were got with child during the dancing, and when they danced they bound and tied themselves around the body so that they became more slender. Upon this some masters, especially the good doctors, said that some got the dancing-sickness who were of a hot nature, and had other natural frailties. There were few of these to whom this happened. The masters of the Holy Scriptures, who exorcised some of the dancers, thought they were possessed by the evil spirit. And so it came to a bad end, and had lasted quite sixteen weeks or thereabouts in these lands. Moreover the aforesaid dancers, men and women, declared that they could not bear the sight of red. And it was nothing but lies, and, in my opinion, a sin against Christ.

As has often been emphasised, the dancing mania and similar phenomena such as flagellant dances or epidemic children's dances (the story of the Pied Piper of Hamelin is a relic of the latter) have a definite connection with the outbreaks of plague and the social miseries of the Middle Ages. One reaction to the hopelessness of life was an overheated religious atmosphere, particularly favourable to the outbreak of hysterical or psychotic manifestations. It is interesting from the sociological point of view that only the lower classes were attacked by dancing mania. We never hear of anyone belonging to a higher class being carried away by it. The movements of the dance were mainly mimed imitations of the work of peasants and artisans.[4]

We have to take our survey from the point of view of religious phenomenology a step further. Discussing the Dionysiac orgies in his work *Die Geburt der Tragödie aus dem Geiste der Musik*, Nietzsche says: 'In Germany too, in the Middle Ages, ever-increasing hordes, in the grip of the same Dionysiac power, moved from place to place, singing and dancing. We can recognise, in these St John's dances and St Vitus's dances, the Bacchic routs of the Greeks, with their pre-history in Asia Minor, going back to Babylon and the orgiastic Sacaea.'[5] This reaches to the heart of the matter. The psychic fringe phenomena, caused in the Middle Ages by the Black Death, hunger and social repression, are in reality the breaking out of old Dionysian forces, driven underground by an Apollonian and Christian culture which was no longer master of the situation. Emerging at last, they offered their own type of redemption. Since they had been disintegrated and thus 'unpractised' for many centuries, they broke out in an uncontrolled and destructive form. It was logical that our text, in common with many other sources, should describe the dancing mania as heresy, caused – as a part of the dancers also believed – by possession 'by the evil spirit'. This is obviously very close to Satan worship.

2 A relic of the ancient Saturnalia is the so-called *Festum fatuorum* (Festival of Fools), celebrated at the New Year from the end of the twelfth century in various places in France, and, in isolated

instances, in other countries too.[6] Its harmless antecedents and parallel forms were the dances of the lower clergy and the children in the church, the *Festum innocentium* (Festival of the Innocents) including the installation of a boy bishop (*episcopus puerorum*),[7] the *Festum hypodiaconorum*, and so on. The Festival of Fools went on up to the beginning of the sixteenth century. Here is a passage from a work by the Archbishop of Sens, written in 1445.

Ludovicus archiepiscopus Senonensis in Stat. ann. 1445, Inter Instr., tom. 12, Gall. Christ., col. 96, (Du Cange IV, p. 484)

You may well tremble and blush when you see the wicked rites of a certain festival the organisers of which call it the Feast of Fools. The tradition is without a doubt the work of the Devil, but it has been handed down to priests and clerics in many churches as something to be observed under the venerable name of the Lord and in joyful celebration of the days of his birth. At a time when they ought to be striving for complete sanctity, they give themselves over to filth and indecency at the hour of divine service. Wearing masks with hideous features, and dressed like women, pimps[a] or actors, they dance in the church and choir, sing indecent songs, eat rich sweets off a corner of the altar next to the celebrant of the Mass, or play dice in the same place. For incense they use stinking smoke made by burning the leather of old shoes. They run and they leap through the whole church, not blushing for their shame, and carry naked men, with even their private parts uncovered, through town and public places in dirty chariots and carts. They put on infamous shows to win the laughter of bystanders and those who flock to see them, twisting their bodies into disgusting postures, uttering shameless and scurrilous words, and committing other abominations shameful to remember, and this appalling fornication is justly called the Feast of Fools, that is, an assembly of evil men rejoicing in the most evil of practices.

The Feast of Fools, called in the text 'without a doubt the work of the Devil', is a reaction against the Apollonian light, dignity and nobility of the ecclesiastical cult. We must not lose sight of the

[a]This could also be read in the Latin text as *leonum* (lions). cf. the letter from the Faculty of Theology at Paris dated 12 March 1444.

fact that those who participated in these festivals were devout followers of the Church, who dutifully attended divine service on all the other days of the year. Only once in the year did they claim a fool's freedom, and parody the liturgy and the church processions. Here too, Dionysiac and anti-spiritual forces are at work. A French miniature of the fifteenth century shows this sort of scene: dancers, naked flagellants and drunkards are seen in front of a church, perhaps after a burial.[8] A bishop is saying: 'They have sacrificed to devils and not to God.'

The Church to some extent understood these practices, which had their part in spiritual 'hygiene'. The milder forms of such customs were expressly tolerated (see above). 'Carnival', too, has to be mentioned in this context.

Certain rites which did not form part of the normal cult were even regulated by the Church. A particularly interesting one is the ball-game in Auxerre cathedral. It was played by the Bishop and his clergy on a floor mosaic in the form of a maze (this is a Dionysian motif) to the accompaniment of the Easter sequence *Victimae paschali laudes*. The rules of the monastery of Auxerre for the year 1396 contain one relating to the game. The custom is attested as late as 1538.[9]

3 The Feast of Asses (*Festum asinorum*)[10] is related to the Feast of Fools. It originated in memory of the Flight into Egypt. In France it gave rise to a peculiar ritual. A donkey, ridden by a girl – probably representing Mary – was led into the church in solemn procession to the accompaniment of all kinds of practical jokes. When the ass had taken its place on the north side of the altar, the service began. We quote a portion of the rubric and some of the Ass's Hymn from the mass, taken from a fourteenth-century manuscript describing the Feast of Asses in Beauvais:

Rubricus et Hymnus inter Missarum solemnia, Bellovaci die 14 Januarii., MS codex XIV. s. (Du Cange III, p. 461)

At the end of the Mass the priest, turning to the congregation, instead of the 'Ite, missa est', shall bray three times, and the people, instead of the 'Deo gratias', shall reply three times, 'Hee-haw, hee-haw, hee-haw'.

From Eastern regions
The Ass has come
Handsome and very strong
Most fitted to bear burdens.

Hey, sir Ass, sing!
Refuse titbits,
You shall have enough hay
And plenty of oats.

God from Arabia,
Frankincense and myrrh from Sheba,
Have been brought into the church
By the power of the Ass.

Hey, sir Ass, etc.

Say Amen, Ass
(here they kneel)
You can eat your fill of grass;
Amen, repeat Amen;
You can reject the old.[a]
Gee-up, gee-up, gee-up!

To ancient peoples the ass[11] was on the one hand a noble, even a holy and prophetic beast, and on the other hand a symbol of evil and darkness. In Greece it was the mount of Dionysus and his followers. 'The unbridled sexuality for which it is notorious made it natural that it should appear in Dionysus' band . . . and the vase pictures show vigorous portrayals of this character.'[12] Similarly with the Romans, the ass was a popular sacrifice to the god Priapus. Christian tradition sees the ass as a symbol (as in the explanation of the story of Christ's entry into Jerusalem), but also of stupidity and the lusts of the flesh. On the well-known mock crucifix of the Palatine, scratched by a Roman soldier on the wall of a guard-room in the Emperor's palace at the beginning of the third century, the crucified figure has an ass's head. Beside it is a gnostic secret sign (Y) and the words, in mockery of a Christian comrade, 'Alexamenos prays to his God'. (Compare the 'Ass's litany' and the 'Ass's feast' that follows it in Nietzsche's *Also sprach*

[a]That is to say old fodder.

Zarathustra[13].) In the Middle Ages the ass was often mentioned in a satanic or demonic context.

At the Feast of Asses the priest and congregation, through their cry of 'Hee-haw', identify themselves with the ass, which is addressed as 'Sire'. The much-glorified 'power of the Ass' appears to have an almost magical effect. In accordance with what we have said about the symbolism of the animal, this power is to be regarded as an instinctive force. The cult of Dionysus, driven underground by the Church, comes to light in the *Festum Asinorum*, particularly in its instinctive aspect. I am not in a position to judge whether the participants' identification with the ass is interesting also from a sociological point of view (as an identification with a beast of burden which shows extreme strength).

B *Satanic cult-forms of medieval heretics*

We are now approaching the Satan cult proper. We should begin by listing the Satanic cult-forms used by medieval heretics, but this is extremely difficult because scholars have not yet been able to form a clear picture of medieval sects,[14] and so far we have no useful research in this field to draw upon. We cannot undertake a historical survey; that is a task for historians. We shall confine ourselves to selecting a few particularly interesting documents from those available.[15]

The heretical movements of the Middle Ages were, through Manicheism,[16] very strongly influenced by the dualistic ideas of Gnosticism. The evil demiurge, the 'Archon of this world' of the Gnostics, was identified with the Christians' Satan, and the concept soon developed of Satan as the evil adversary of God or as the son of the evil God.[17] The kingdoms of the good and evil gods are in eternal and implacable opposition to each other. This extreme dualism led to a rigidly spiritualistic attitude, a radical rejection of everything earthly. The heretics' satanic rites, in which sexual acts are usually of prime importance, are all the more surprising. Even if a considerable part of the information given in the sources is calumny, they contain a nucleus of historical truth. How can this contradiction be explained?

The paradox rests on various interpretations.[18] It was believed that sin could be most easily overcome if it was killed by sin. Or that the truly pure ('Katharos' or 'Catharus') could without fear come into contact with the world and the flesh, and thus with Satanism. He could rise above it and not be contaminated. On the contrary, the pure could even turn evil into good, so that, for example, all with whom the 'Perfect' came into sexual contact would be healed. The interpretation of the source documents will show on what practical basis this theory can be supposed to rest.

1 The most important early source, continually referred to in later times, consists of the acts of the Synod of Orleans of 1022. It refers to the religious practices of the neo-Manichaeans, a movement which reached Orleans from the south of France before 1019.[19]

Gesta Synodi Aurelianensis an. MXXII [on dating see Borst, op. cit. (note 14), p. 76, note 13] *adversus novos Manichaeos (Bouquet X, p. 538)*

. . . They assembled on certain nights in the appointed house, each holding a lantern in his hand. They called out the names of the demons like a litany, until suddenly they saw a demon descend among them in the form of some animal. At once all the lights were put out, so that that vision could be clearly seen, and everyone, as quickly as he could, seized whatever woman came to hand and abused her, without thinking of the sin, or whether he was possessing their mother, or sister, or a nun; and they considered that intercourse to be something sacred and religious. And if in that filthy intercourse a child was begotten, a great fire was lit on the eighth day, and it was tried by fire according to the custom of the ancient heathen, and so burnt. Its ashes were collected with great reverence, and kept, as pious Christians keep the body of Christ, to give them as a viaticum to the sick on the point of death. There was such power of diabolical trickery in those ashes that anyone taking even a little of those ashes could scarcely ever afterwards forsake that heresy and walk in the ways of truth.

Even at first glance we can see the resemblance to the Gnostic feast of the Phibionites (see above, p. 25ff); but here the accent is on the sexual act itself. This is seen by the assembly as *pro sanctitate et religione* – something sacred and religious. The sexual act is an orgy in which there are no barriers even to incest.

Religious orgies occur among many races.[20] Sometimes they are magical fertility rites, but in most cases they have different significance. The orgy can be considered as direct possession by a supernatural power manifesting itself in sex, or as a return to a state of Paradise or an anticipation of such a return in the future, but also as a purification or liberation from all that is earthly, personal or sensual – a release from captivity through instinctive drives. The rite we have just considered must surely be taken in this latter sense, if we consider the participants' dualistic conception of the world. The aim is thus 'a catharsis and a cleansing of the soul; a reorganisation of all the levels of the empirical consciousness through sexuality'.[21] The 'pure' becomes still purer through the orgy, and sexuality is the medium through which he is cleansed. The sensual is transformed into the spiritual. In other words, the orgy here becomes a rite of ecstatic liberation and rebirth. As this rite is centred on a demon appearing in animal form (a symbol of primitive instinct), it is Satanic in character. However, unlike the witches' sabbath of the late Middle Ages, this appears by the procedure to be only a 'temporary' Satanism. To some extent the assembly regards the Satanic sexuality represented by the demon as a mere 'springboard' to purity and perfection.

The prevention and rejection of children must be considered in relation to the ethics of the Gnostics. The kingdom of the prince of this world must not be increased. The ashes of the murdered child are important. According to a widespread belief, the ashes contain the essence of a life. Besides their medicinal effectiveness, they have magic power and are often used in spells.[22] Their 'mana' is due especially to the fact that the child, 'tried' by the fire, left the prison of earthly life by a path that was the prototype of the Redemption, and so had become a 'saint'. The eating of the ashes is thus a mystical act which binds the communicants still more closely to the religious fellowship.

The neo-Manichaeans of Orleans were the first heretics in the western world to be condemned to be burnt at the stake. Laughing, as the sources tell us, they went to their deaths on 28 December 1022.[23]

2 The following account of heretical rites by Guibert de Nogent dates from the early twelfth century:

Guibert de Nogent, De vita sua III, 17, (Migne PL, CLVI, 951)

They hold their meetings in hidden vaults or inner rooms; they make no distinction between the sexes. Lighting candles they offer them from behind to a harlot bending forward with naked buttocks, as they say, for everyone to see. Then putting out the candles they proclaim chaos everywhere, and every man copulates with the woman who comes first to hand.

If a woman becomes pregnant there, she returns there as soon as the birth is over.

A great fire is lit, and they sit round it and throw the child from hand to hand through the flames until the fire is out. Then it is reduced to ashes, and bread is made from the ashes. Part of it is distributed for the Eucharist; once they have eaten it they almost never turn away from that heresy.

The rite with the candles is unusual. The harlot, whom some cultures see as rich in mana because of her aura of impersonal eroticism, appears as a kind of female demon to whom candles – clearly phallic symbols – are offered. The buttocks, to which the offering is directed, are considered in the ancient symbolism of the body as the zone of the Devil and of Hell. The offering of the candles as a preliminary to the religious ceremony is a symbolic marriage with a figure representing the primitive Satanic impulse in its feminine aspect. The rest corresponds almost exactly to the Orleans source.

3 Reports from Germany about heretical sects in the north-west of that country (the town in question was Staden) led Pope Gregory IX, a particularly ardent persecutor of heretics, to issue the decretal *Vox in rama* in 1233. We quote the description of the ritual:

Gregory IX: Decretal 'Vox in rama', 13 June 1233, to King Henry VII. (Parallel letters to Archbishop Siegfried III of Mainz and Bishop Conrad of Hildesheim), (Mansi, vol. 23, cols 324f (Potthast, No. 9229 and 9230))

For when a novice is received into it [the community], and enters their meeting rooms for the first time, he sees a kind of frog, called by some a toad. Some kiss this beast in damnable fashion on the rump, some on the mouth, taking its tongue and its saliva into their own mouths. This animal sometimes appears of unusual size, sometimes as big as a goose or a duck, and often it is the size of an oven. As the novice goes on he meets a man of strange pallor, with very dark eyes, so lean and emaciated that he looks as though all his flesh had melted away leaving only the skin stretched over the bones. The novice kisses him, and feels him as cold as ice, and after the kiss the memory of the Catholic faith completely fades from his heart. A little later, they sit down to a meal, and when it is over, they get up from the table. Then, from a statue which normally stands in their meeting room, a black cat, as large as a medium-sized dog, comes down backwards, with tail raised. First the novice, then the master, then the others in order, but only the worthy and perfect, kiss it on its rump. But the imperfect, who are not deemed worthy, receive the kiss of peace from the master. When all the others are in their places, and have uttered certain chants, with their heads inclined towards the cat, the master says 'per se nobis'. The next man answers: 'Who commands this?', a third says 'The supreme master', and a fourth 'we must obey him'. And when this is done the candles are put out, and they go on to the most disgusting work of lechery with no distinction made between strangers and close kindred. If by chance some men are left, over and above the number of women, the passions of shame are not abated in them; they burn with lust one for another, and men commit fornication upon men. Women too change their natural desires, and, completely against nature, do the same damnable thing. When this utterly disgusting crime has been completed, and the candles relit, and all are back in their places, from a dark corner of the room, where there is no lack of utterly depraved men, a man comes out, glowing above the hips and brighter than the sun, as they say – although below he is like a stupid cat – and his brightness illuminates the whole place. Then the master, tearing off something from the novice's garments, says to this glittering apparition: 'Master, I give to thee what has been given to me.' And the glittering man replies: 'Thou hast served me well, and shalt serve me better; I commit to thy care that which thou hast given me.' And with these words he at once vanishes. They also take the body of Christ from the priest's hand at Easter every year, and they carry it home in their mouths and throw it into the privy as an insult to the Redeemer.

The text describes an initiation ceremony (on the initiation see below, p. 83). Satan appears first to the novice in the shape of a frog or toad. Because of its extraordinary fertility and its connection with both water and earth – the elements of life – the frog has become in many places, such as in ancient Egypt and among the Coptic Christians, a symbol of renewal and rebirth.[24] But it can also be an object of disgust and a symbol of evil and impurity (see Exod. 8: 2ff and Rev. 16: 13). In the Christian tradition the frog appears very early as an image of the Devil, since, it is said,[25] it lives in the slime, that is, the lowest depths of sensuality. The size of the frog, mentioned in the text, emphasises the importance of this apparition of the Devil. The frog's rump, which is ritually kissed, brings into relief the chthonic aspect of the animal symbol. The taking in of the saliva refers to the old belief that saliva contains mysterious life-forces and is to be considered as the sap of life.[26]

In the further course of the initiation ceremony Satan appears as a pale, emaciated man, ice-cold to the touch – a being, then, largely deprived of the substance of life. This makes sense insofar as it is the pictorial image of the Devil which is current in the Christian world. At the ritual feast Satan's metamorphoses continue. The cat is a favourite symbol for the Devil,[27] both because of its black colour and its sexual aggressiveness. The kissing rite corresponds to the custom of the kiss of peace at the mass. After some ritual responses (which are not very clear in the original text), the orgy again follows. Here the homosexual side is stressed; as the only reason given is the inequality of numbers between men and women, it confirms the fact that this is not intercourse between the sexes but a sexual *actus purus* – the sexual act for its own sake.

Finally Satan changes into a hybrid being; the lower half of his body remains that of a cat, but the upper half is that of a man, 'glowing . . . and brighter than the sun'. This is an obvious parallel with Jesus transfigured on the mountain (Matt. 17: 1f, Mark 9: 3, Luke 9: 29). There is also a kind of synthesis between the figure of Christ and the figure of Satan. This produces a symbol of one single entity, which is very rare in the cult of Satan. The rite with the torn-off piece of clothing symbolises the dedication of the initiate, perfected through the mediation of the master of the assembly.

The full significance of the custom of throwing the host into the privy can only be measured if we reemember that the Satan worshippers were firmly convinced of the priest's power of consecration and of the actual presence of Christ in the elements of the Eucharist. It is only because the adherents of Satanic cults clung to this Christian belief right up to the nineteenth century that their blasphemous actions have their full weight.

We must emphasise once again that the question of how far the allegedly Satanic rites of the heretics are historically substantiated is irrelevant to our purpose. Even the mere imaginings of their accusers have a reality which must be taken seriously from both the phenomenological and the psychological point of view. We must add that the sociological aspect of the heretical movements[28] could not be considered here.

C *The ritual of the witches' sabbath*

Some isolated elements of the witches' sabbath, particularly flight, are found as early as the ninth century; but its peculiar ritual took shape in the fourteenth and fifteenth centuries, and it was not until the sixteenth that the 'sabbath', as the late medieval demonologists called it for short, became a permanent feature of the witches' existence. It reached its final peculiar form in that century and at the beginning of the seventeenth.[29]

The *Dictionnaire Infernal* of J. Collin de Plancy gives the following definition of the sabbath. 'It is the assembly of demons, wizards and witches in their nightly orgies.'[30] Besides 'sabbath' (in the general meaning of the Hebrew *schabbath* – 'festival'), the term 'synagogue of Satan' – referring to Rev. 2: 9 and 3: 9 – or simply 'synagogue' came into use.

The classic breeding-ground for the medieval witch cult was the south of France, the meeting-place of the currents of Jewish-cabbalistic occult sciences and Islamic and Moorish magic from Spain with Christianity. The cult of the witches' sabbath spread from this centre over a great part of Europe, taking on many additions from local folklore as it went.

It is almost impossible to survey all the wealth of source documents on the witches' sabbath. In any case we meet for the most part with endless wearisome repetitions, to be accounted for by the rigidly unvarying procedure of the witch-trials, or with equally boring pseudo-philosophical treatises. Only comparatively few documents are really interesting. We are selecting three of these: the first, a Spanish text dated 1610, gives one of the most detailed descriptions of the sabbath that we possess. The second contains extracts from a book that appeared a few years later, by the famous demonologist de Lancre, whom Michelet, differing from the majority of inquisitors, called *un homme d'esprit*.[31] The third, dated 1623, adds substantially to our knowledge of the phenomenon.

1 Under the influence of emigrants from the French Basque country, who had fled from the marsh inquisition of that same de Lancre, a witch panic broke out in 1609 in the Spanish town of Logrono on the upper Ebro. Although at that time the 'Suprema', the highest authority of the Spanish Inquisition, was reluctant to occupy itself with witch trials (as distinct from trials for heresy) and even restrained over-eager local authorities from undertaking witch hunts, they felt bound to act in this case. In November 1610 a solemn *auto-da-fé* was set up in Logrono, at which six witches were burnt, eighteen recanted and were pardoned, and five died in prison.[32]

We quote from the report of the *auto-da-fé* (Biblioteca Nacional, Madrid) the most important passages relating to the witches' sabbath:

Relacion de las personas que salieron al Auto de la fee, que los senores Doctor Alonso Bezerra Holguin, del Abito de Alcantara: Licenciado Iuan de Valle Albarado: Licenciado Alonso de Salazar Frias, Inquisadores Apostolicos, del Reyno de Navarra, y su distrito, celebraron en la Ciudad de Logrono, en siete, y en ocho dias del mes de Noviembre, de 1610 Anos

Account of the incidents and the evil deeds which took place in the sect of witches as reported in the declarations and confessions.

The Devil, to propagate this abominable and accursed sect, uses the oldest and most experienced sorcerers, who take great pains to become masters and teachers of the art. Those whom they persuade to be witches cannot be taken to the Witches' Sabbath (which is the name they give to their meetings and assemblies; and in Basque they also speak of the Goat's Meadow, because the Devil, whom they look upon as their god and lord, very commonly appears to them at all their sabbaths in the form of a goat) until they first consent to become witches, and having reached years of discretion promise to make renunciation [of the Christian faith]. And when someone has consented and promised, the master who has taught him and persuaded him to become a witch comes on the night of a Sabbath, two or three hours before midnight, to his bed, or wherever he is sleeping or awake, wakes him if he is asleep, and with a greenish-black, foul-smelling water anoints his hands, temples, breast, private parts, and soles of the feet, and then takes him with him through the air, pulling him through the doors or windows which the Devil opens for them, or through some other crack or through the keyhole, and with great speed and in great haste they reach the Sabbath, and the place appointed for the meeting. Then the master presents the novice witch to the Devil, who is seated on a throne which sometimes appears to be of gold and sometimes of black wood, with great dignity, majesty and gravity, and with a very sad, ugly and bad-tempered face (he then shows himself as a black man with a crown of little horns, and three of them are very large and like a goat's horns; two he wears on the back of his head and the other on his forehead, and with these he sheds a glow and lights up everyone at the Sabbath, and the light is greater than that of the moon, but much less than that of the sun; and it is enough to make everything clear and recognisable). His eyes are round, large, wide open, glowing and terrible. His beard is like a goat's. His body and form are midway between those of a man and a goat; his hands and feet have fingers and toes like a man's, except that they are all the same length and taper to a point, with sharp talons, and his hands are curved like the claws of a bird of prey, and his feet are like those of a gander. And he has a terrible, discordant voice, and when he speaks it sounds like an owl screeching, but one with a deep voice, and the words he utters are badly pronounced, so that they cannot be clearly heard, and he always speaks in a sad, hoarse voice as though he were always unhappy, and his appearance is very melancholy, and he seems always irritable. And when the Chief Witch presents the novice to him, she says 'Lord, I bring this man to you and present him to you.' And the Devil shows himself to be pleased, and says he will treat him well in order that many more may come with him. And then they make the novice bend the knee before the Devil, and renounce [Christianity] in the same way and the same particulars as the witch his teacher has impressed upon him. The Devil tells him the words of renunciation, and he repeats them, denying first God, then Saint Mary the Virgin his Mother, then all the saints, baptism and confirmation, both the Chrisms, [the ordination of priests and Extreme Unction] his godfathers and godmothers, the Faith and all Christians; and he receives as his Lord and God the Devil, who tells him that from then onward he must not take the God of the Christians as his Lord and God, but only him, the true Lord and God, who can save him and take him to Paradise. And then he receives him as his Lord and God and worships him, kissing his left hand, his mouth, his breast near his heart, and his private parts, and he [the Devil] turns on his left side, and lifts his tail (which is like that of an ass) and uncovers the parts of his body that are very ugly, and he always keeps them dirty and very stinking, and he is kissed there too, under the tail. And then the Devil stretches out his left hand, and puts it down over his [the novice's] head on to his left shoulder or other different parts of the body (as he may wish) and makes a mark by piercing him with one of his claws so as to make a wound from which blood flows. This he collects on a cloth or in a vessel; and the new witch feels very great pain from the wound, which lasts for more than a month, and the mark or sign lasts all his life. . . .

On the eve of certain main festivals of the year – the three days of Easter, the Epiphany, the Ascension, Corpus Christi, All Saints, Candlemas, the Assumption, the Nativity of Our Lady, and the feast of St John the Baptist, they assemble for the Witches' Sabbath, solemnly to worship the Devil, and they all confess to him, taking as sins the number of times they have entered the church or heard Mass, and everything else they have done like Christians, and the evil deeds they might have done but have not. And the Devil rebukes them sternly and says they must do nothing like the Christians. And meanwhile the servants of the Devil (who are other devils of the same shape and form as the one of the Witches' Sabbath, though smaller; there are usually six or seven of them, and when they are required they appear there in great numbers) set up an altar with an old black cloth, ugly and worn, as an altar-cloth, and upon it some images of the Devil, chalice, host, missal, vessels for the wine, and some garments like those used in the Church to say Mass (except that these are black, ugly and dirty) and the Devil robes himself with the help of his servants, and they serve his Mass, singing with deep, hoarse and discordant voices. And he sings [Mass] from a book like a missal which appears to be of stone, and preaches them a sermon in which he tells them not to be vainglorious and recognise other gods than him, who can save them and take them to Paradise; and though in this life they will suffer travail and need, he will give them great comfort in the other world, if they only do as much harm to Christians as they can. And then he continues his Mass, and they bring him the offertory, and he sits to receive it on a black throne placed there for him, and the eldest and most important witch (the Queen of the Sabbath) takes her place beside him, with a pyx in her hand on which a portrait of the Devil is painted, and in the other hand a little basin like those used in churches to collect for the lights to burn in front of the saints; she has a chain like gold round her neck, on every link of which the face of the Devil is enamelled. And all the witches, in order of importance, bring each their own offering, making three curtsies to the Devil with the left foot, until their knees touch the ground; and they kiss the image of the Devil on the pyx, and throw into the basin the money they have brought to offer . . . and as they throw it into the basin, they say, 'This is for the honour of the world and the glory of the feast.' And the women too offer loaves of bread, eggs and other things which are received by the Devil's servants, and then they kneel down beside him and kiss his left hand and his breast near the heart, and two witches who hold the office of train-bearers lift up his skirts so that they can kiss him in his private parts, and as the Devil turns on his left side, they lift up his tail and uncover the parts which are very dirty and stinking; and at the moment when they kiss him under his tail, he lets out a gust of wind with a very horrible smell; he does this almost every time anyone kisses him there. And after the offertory he continues his Mass, and he lifts up a round thing like the sole of a shoe, on which the figure of the Devil is painted, saying 'This is my body', and all the witches kneel and worship him, beating their breasts and saying *Aquerragoyti*, *Aquerrakeyti*, which means 'Goat up, goat down'. And they do the same when he lifts up the cup, which is made of a kind of black ugly wood, and is like the host, and drinks what is in the cup. And then all the witches form into a circle, and he gives them communion, giving each a black fragment (on which the figure of the Devil is painted) which is very harsh and unpleasant to swallow; and then he also gives them a sip of a very bitter liquid, and as they drink their hearts grow very cold.

When the Devil has finished his Mass, he copulates with everyone, men and women, carnally and after the fashion of Sodom. The aforesaid Graciana de Barrenechea, the Queen [of the Sabbath] went round indicating those witches who had to go where the Devil was, a little apart, for the same purpose. And Estebania de Iriarte, her daughter, was the one who went most often to perform those acts; and when her said mother signalled to her to go there, Joanes de Goyburu her [the mother's] husband (who played the tambourine, with Joanes de Sansin on the drum) went to the place where the witches were standing, and took her out from among them, and conducted her with music to the place where the Devil was. He, with his left hand (in the sight of everyone) stretched her face downwards on the ground, or placed her against a tree and there had knowledge of her in the manner of the Sodomites, while her said husband Joanes de Sansin made music. And while still in the said act, she gave a very shrill scream which everyone heard; and when they were asked [by the court] what the scream sounded like, they said it was like a bull roaring. And when they had finished the shameful acts she went away very proud and satisfied, and they took her back to the sound of music to the place whence they had taken her. And in the same way the said Queen went round indicating all those who had to go and copulate with the Devil; and they were fetched with the same music and ceremony, and returned to their places, and they all gave the same scream as they finished the shameful act. And the said Maria Iriarte, daughter of the Queen, declares that when her mother sent her for the first time for this purpose, the Devil entered her carnally by both ways, and deflowered her, and she suffered much pain, and returned home with her shift all bloody; and she complained to her mother about it, and she replied that it did not matter, and that he had done the same with her. . . . And Martin Viccar Bruco, a recanting witch (who, at the Sabbath, had held the office of Constable, to control and look after the children) reports that the first time the Devil had knowledge of him after the fashion of Sodom, he suffered great pain, and returned home all bloody, and to satisfy his wife (who asked him what that blood was) he pretended that a branch of a tree had struck him in the leg. And when the Devil had finished these evil acts, and others, very horrible, which shall not be mentioned, the witches copulated one with another, men with women, and men with men, without distinction of rank or kindred . . .

The first part of the text describes the solemn reception of the novice into the community of witches. This initiation ceremony is copied from elements of Christian baptism, which gives it the character of an antithesis to the Christian initiation mysteries. It is interesting that the 'witch sect' – probably under the influence of corresponding usuages in contemporary heretical movements – goes back to a custom of the early Church which at that time had long fallen into disuse: the initiates must have reached the age of discretion before they can be accepted into the religious community. In official Christianity the baptism of infants became customary in the second half of the fourth century; but in the 'witch sect' (the idea of a coherent witch sect took shape in the fifteenth century) it was insisted that the entrants should make their own independent decision. This shows an obvious preference for the so-called *opus operantis*, which means personal involvement in a ceremony, over the so-called *opus operatum*, or pure ritual, and can be considered as a reaction against the late medieval overemphasis on liturgical procedure, which often became purely mechanical.

Before flying to the sabbath, the place of initiation, the master witch anoints the candidate on various parts of his body with a foul-smelling watery fluid. This is not merely an imitation of the Church's anointing ceremonies, but has a very real purpose, since it induces hallucinations, particularly that of flight. According to old recipes, essential ingredients of witches' ointment include the thorn-apple (*Datura stramonium*), henbane (*Hyoscyamus niger*) and deadly nightshade (*Atropa belladonna*).[33] From information given by old writers such as Giambattista della Porta (about 1535–1615) and Johann Weikshand von Valvasor (1641–93) and the experiments of modern scholars such as Hermann Fühner (1925), Siegbert Ferckel (1954) and Will-Erich Peuckert (1960),[34] we know that ointments made from plants of the nightshade family cause the subject to fall into a deep dream-state or delirium. 'First of all, horribly distorted faces danced before my eyes. Then suddenly I had a feeling as though I were flying miles through the air. The flight was repeatedly interrupted by deep downward swoops. In the final phase came the picture of an orgiastic feast with grotesque sensual debauchery' (from an experiment by Peuckert on himself).[35] It is not correct, however, to see all the phenomena of the sabbath as pure hallucination or imagination. It is only with the flight that this is completely the case.

The religion of the Church, being basically Apollonian, leaves the use of drugs severely alone. But at the witches' sabbath these ancient practices, known all over the world, come to life again. As Erich Neumann shows, knowledge of drugs that awaken the unconscious and produce an *abaissement du niveau mental* belongs to the domain of the Great Goddess as Earth Mother and Goddess of the Night.[36] It is women who, at the sabbath, prepare the ointments used by the witch master in the text just quoted. The green colour of the fluid shows that it belongs to the world of vegetative nature, which – by its contrast with the spiritual world – often takes on a demoniac character in Christian folklore; this colour, therefore, is easily associated with the Devil.[37] The novice witch, once anointed, is transported into the matriarchal world of the moon-goddess and of the maenads of Dionysus.

The Devil appears as a goat, or, as here, with a body that is half goat, half man. The Devil in the form of a goat is, as has often been pointed out, the resurrection of the old goat-god Pan, the son of Hermes, who finally developed from an Arcadian shepherd-god to the god of everything, as his name implies. The primitive Pan 'belongs to the world of the nymphs, of wildly proliferating Nature. . . . He flees from domestic man and his social order, and the only relationship he has with him is the occasional terror occasioned by meeting unexpectedly his demonic hybrid form. . . . He is a god evolved from the essence of an animal. . . . The goat is the symbol of the fertility which assures the increase of the herd. So it is quite natural that the god should appear as an active begetter, and then, as he became more human, as an ardent lover and pursuer of women; then, more vulgarised, as a strongly erotic being with the potency and sexual drive of a stud animal.'[38] When Christianity, with its emphasis on the spirit, ceased to recognise wild, fertile nature as divine, the deity that symbolised it became the antithesis of God. Pan, who in the Greece of classical times was already the ruler of the universe, described in an Orphic hymn as 'Glorious, Dancer, God-inspired, All-begetting, Fruit-bearer'[39] became the satanic Pantocrator.

Pan is closely related to Dionysus; some works of art show him in the train of satyrs and maenads, participating in the Dionysian festival of the grape harvest, or as a figure in relief on the buildings of theatres, which were sacred to Dionysus.[40] But Dionysus too has affinities with the goat, even appearing frequently in the myths in the shape of a goat, and such names as 'young goat' or 'the one in the black goatskin' are among the epithets used in his cult. The goat is also an animal preferred by him for sacrifice.[41] It is generally known that in early times the Dionysian choral singers wore masks and costumes of goats, (*tragoi*, whence *tragōdia*). Thus Satan in the form of a goat has also essential Dionysian characteristics.

Besides this Greek and in part Hellenistic tradition, which was passed on through the Roman myths of Faunus and Bacchus, and probably also influenced by Etruscan demon legends,[42] a second source contributed to the figure of the Devil as a goat – Jewish and Biblical folklore. In Palestine the goats were always put into separate folds from the sheep for the night, because of their smell and their lively unpredictability, and so became the symbol of rejection.[43] Thus we have the scapegoat of the Old Testament (Lev. 16: 20ff), while in the New Testament Jesus uses the goat as the image of the damned at the Last Judgement (Math. 25: 32f; cf. Ezekiel 34: 17). Those participating in the witches' sabbath must have been particularly familiar with this Biblical symbolism. Satan's goat-shape provided an antithesis to traditional ideas of divinity that must have been comprehensible even to the masses.

As in all descriptions of the sabbath, great stress is laid in our text on Satan's horns. Besides a crown of small horns, he has three long ones, of which the one on his forehead is a source of light. The horn was already important in prehistoric times, in the ancient Near East and in Crete, and it plays a great part in the Bible. Because of its importance as an offensive and defensive weapon as well as a phallic symbol, it symbolises victory and superior strength.[44] In antithesis to the seven horns of the Lamb of God (Rev. 5: 6), the Dragon of the Apocalypse and the beast from the sea have ten horns (Rev. 12: 3, 13: 2) and the beast from the land two horns (Rev. 13: 11). This is also the meaning of the Devil's horns. The light-shedding horn is a concrete reminder of his name – Lucifer. (It is of interest in this context that occasionally in the

Old Testament the word 'horn' is used for 'ray of light' and 'horned' for 'radiant'.)[45]

Despite his attributes of power, Satan appears as a being 'with a very sad face', as 'bad-tempered', as speaking 'with a sad voice', as 'much melancholic' and 'always irritable'. This gives him specifically human characteristics, so that he is described as a dark man. But his mixture of absolute ambition and ill humour gives him what the text calls '*arrogance*'. His sadness and irritability are explained when we remember his fate as a creature despised and rejected by God and the Christian world. In psychological terms this is a depressive state which, as experience shows, arises from a situation of rejection and is characterised by the discrepancy between a turmoil of overweening ambition and its complete lack of fulfilment. From this point of view the witches' sabbath may be seen as a mighty effort on Satan's part to free himself by sorcery from his painful depression – an effort which, as always happens with depressives, changes nothing, and leaves him in exactly the same situation as before.[46]

The renunciation of God, the Virgin Mary, all the saints and the sacraments of the Church is imitated from the *abrenuntiatio* of the baptismal service. After the rite of the kiss (see below, p. 83) the novice receives from Satan the indelible witch mark. Here too there is a parallel with Church usage; according to Catholic doctrine the initiation mysteries of baptism and confirmation leave a mark in the soul, that is, 'a certain spiritual and indelible sign' (*characterem in anima, hoc est signum quoddam spirituale et indelebile*).[47] The vital difference is that the mark made by Satan is not only spiritual, but physical at the same time, and that its setting is attended with great pain. There is an obvious parallel with the initiation ceremonies of primitive races.[48] This again shows the anti-spiritual trend of the Satan cult. The Devil's use of his left hand to make the mark is connected with the ancient association of the right side with good and the left with evil.[49]

The second part of the text describes the sabbath itself. It is introduced by a distorted version of the confession, after which the black mass is celebrated. In construction it follows the Roman liturgy, and it is interesting that in certain parts the older forms of the latter are preserved. The Satanic version of the kiss of peace comes before the offertory, as it formerly did in the Roman mass, according to the words of the Sermon on the Mount (Math. 5:

23f). (Later, without any obvious reason, it was moved to the end of the Eucharist.)[50] The rite of the bringing of gifts follows a very early tradition, lost long before the late Middle Ages. It occurs in the form of the once customary procession,[51] and other provisions besides bread are brought to the altar – a usage provided for in the liturgy of St Hippolytus, dating from the year 200.[52] The offertory of the black mass reacts in this way against the completely individual and spiritual practice of the later Church. While the consecration is a direct perversion of the well-known liturgical act, the communion goes back to the lay chalice, which was generally used before the thirteenth century. The meaning of the 'Queen of the Sabbath' and the sexual orgies following the black mass will be discussed when we examine the next source documents.

2 Pierre de Lancre, born in Bordeaux in 1553, a member of the council of his home town, was sent by King Henry IV to Labourd, a district in the western Pyrenees bordering on Spain, to inquire into the question of witchcraft; he was given the appointment because he spoke the Basque language. He started his activities at the beginning of the year 1609, and in a short time he had accounted for a large number of witches, although he met with fierce resistance and revolt. Since de Lancre even had some clerics burnt or imprisoned, the Bishop of Bayonne turned against him, and after four months the witch hunt had to be abandoned.[53]

De Lancre is thus the embodiment of secular justice. We quote the following text from his extraordinarily interesting work *Tableau de l'Inconstance* . . . , which did not appear until 1612:

Pierre de Lancre, Tableau de l'Inconstance des mauvais Anges et Démons, Paris 1612. Description of the Sabbath . . . (2nd edn, 1613, pp. 188ff)

The Sabbath is like a fair with a motley crowd of mad, raving merchants arriving from every direction. A meeting and a mixture of a hundred thousand creatures arriving suddenly and passing swiftly, novel, it is true, but with a terrible novelty that offends the eye and sickens the heart. Of these creatures, some are real, and others tricks and illusions; some are pleasant (but very few) like the bells and sweet-sounding instruments, all sorts of which can be heard, which only titillate the ear and do not reach the heart, consisting rather in noise that deafens and alarms than in pleasant soothing harmony. Others are unpleasant, deformed and horrible, tending only towards dissolution, privation, ruin and destruction. Where people become brutalised and turn into animals, losing their speech as long as they are in that state; and animals, on the other hand, speak, and seem to have more sense than people, and each is alienated from his own nature.

The general couriers of the Sabbath are the women, and its mysteries pass through their hands [rather] than through those of the men. They run and fly, as dishevelled as the Furies, according to the custom of the country; their heads are so light that they cannot bear any covering on them. They are seen naked, sometimes oiled, sometimes not. They come and go (for each has some unholy and evil commission) perched on a stick or broom, or carried by a goat or other animal, with a poor child or two mounted behind, and the Devil, now in front as guide, now behind to wield a brutal whip. And when Satan wants to transport them through the air (which is only given to the most adept) he gives them flight and launches them like burning rockets, and when they come down, they arrive at the place appointed, and swoop down a hundred times faster than an eagle or a hawk could swoop upon its prey . . .

The Devil, sovereign master of the assembly, sometimes appears as a stinking bearded goat – of all animals, the ugliest and most horrible form he could have borrowed, and the one with which man has least contact. Sometimes he is seen there as a terrifying tree-trunk shaped like a dark and monstrous man. . . .

If he appears there as a man, it is as a tortured, agonised man, red and flaming as the fire that leaps from a fiery furnace. A blurred outline of a man, only half visible, with a voice that is broken, hoarse and inarticulate, yet imperious, loud and terrible. He is such that it is impossible, seeing him, to say for certain whether he is a man, a tree-trunk or a beast. He sits on a throne which appears to be gold, but flaming; at his side the Queen of the Sabbath, who is a witch he has seduced, to whom he gives an appearance of magnificence; she is adorned with many false jewels, and crowned as a queen to entice the others. He also gives a horrible aspect to almost all those who are present in this accursed assembly, whose faces, in the deceptive light of the pitch candles that are seen there, appear shadowed, grim or veiled; and people seem monstrous in bulk and height, or strangely and unnaturally tiny. . . .

Great cauldrons are seen there, full of toads and vipers, hearts of unbaptised children, flesh of hanged men, and other horrible carrion, and stinking water, pots of grease and poison, which are lent and distributed at this fair. . . .

The women and girls with whom he [the Devil] desires to copulate are covered with a cloud, to hide the shameful and disgusting things which take place, and to avoid the pity which might be felt at the cries and the agonies of these poor wretches. And he seeks to add impiety to the abomination of sorcery, in order to make them think that he wants them to live with some form of religion. The divine service or cult which he tries to imitate or represent is so wild and disorderly, and outside the bounds of reason, that the false celebrant, having set up an altar, pretends to say some form of Mass to make mock of the Christians. And he exhibits there some sort of host, made of some stinking stuff, black and smoky, on which he is depicted as a goat. This false priest, head downwards and feet up, with his back shamefully turned towards the altar. . . .

Marie de la Ralde, aged twenty-eight years, a very beautiful woman . . . says that she did not think she was doing any harm by going to the Sabbath, and that she had much more pleasure and satisfaction there than by going to Mass, because the Devil made them believe that he was the true God, and that the joy that the witches felt at the Sabbath was only the beginning of a much greater glory, when [the Devil] cast down the Lord and uttered several blasphemies to him. . . .

Jeannette d'Abadie, living in Siboro, aged sixteen years . . . said that she saw there the Devil in the shape of a black and hideous man, with six horns on his head, sometimes eight, and a great tail behind, one face in front of his head and another behind, as the god Janus is portrayed; that the said Gratianne [a witch], having presented her, received a large handful of gold in recompense. Then he made her renounce and deny her Creator, the Holy Virgin, the saints, baptism, father, mother, parents, Heaven and Earth and everything in the world; he made her renew this renunciation every time she went to the Sabbath, then she went and kissed his behind. The Devil often made her kiss his face, then his navel, then his member, then his behind. She had often seen children baptised at the Sabbath; these, she explained, were the children of witches and of no others; they preferred to have their children baptised at the Sabbath rather than at church, and to present them to the Devil rather than to God. . . .

As for the coupling [she said], that she saw everybody having incestuous intercourse against all the dictates of nature. . . . She accused herself of having been deflowered by Satan and having had intercourse an infinite number of times with a relative of hers and with others who had condescended to demand her. She shrank from intercourse with the Devil because, as his member was covered with scales, it caused extreme pain, besides which his seed is extremely cold, so that it never makes a woman pregnant, nor does that of the other men at the Sabbath, even though it is natural [sperm]. Outside the Sabbath she never did anything wrong, but at the Sabbath she had a marvellous delight in this intercourse, apart from that with Satan, which she said was horrible. She even seemed to us to take a marvellous delight in telling it and talking about, calling everything by its name more freely and boldly than we dared ask of her, which is a wonderful confirmation of the reality of the Sabbath. For it is more probable that she copulated at the Sabbath with the people she named than that Satan made them appear to her in her bed by illusion, or that he carried them physically to her; she would not have been able to feel this natural sperm a hundred times (as she says) except by copulating physically and actually with a real man whom she named to us, and who is still alive.

[She says] that she has seen the tables laid with much food, but when you tried to take some you found nothing in your hand, except when they had brought baptised or unbaptised children, for she had very often seen both of these served up and eaten. . . . They cut them in quarters at the Sabbath so as to share them among several parishes.

She says further that she had seen several little demons without arms lighting a great fire, throwing in witches from the Sabbath and pulling them out without pain; and the Devil said they would have no more pain from the fires of Hell. . . .

She has seen witches turn themselves into wolves, dogs, cats and other animals, by washing their hands in water they had in a pot, and taking back their own form whenever they wanted to. This happened at the Sabbath, on the way, and anywhere; and while they were transformed they could not be seen, and only a gleam of light could be seen near them.

At great festivals there are general assemblies of witches; she once saw twelve thousand on the coast at Underalse near Hendaye. They hold a sort of council at which it is resolved only that each will do as much harm as he can, and for this purpose poisons and powders are distributed to each of them.

And several others have told us that the pleasure and joy there are so great and so various that there is not a man or a woman that does not go very willingly. Only the children are afraid at all, and then only the very small ones who look after the toads. The wife takes her pleasure in the presence of her husband without suspicion or jealousy, in fact he is often the pander; the father deflowers his daughter without shame; the mother deprives her son of his virginity and the brother his sister; fathers and mothers are seen bringing their children to present them. Finally, at the great assemblies on annual festivals, so many people come and go at the Sabbath from all parts of the earth, that one told us she had seen as many people as there were stars in the sky. They did not think, therefore, that it was a bad thing to go to the Sabbath, but rather that it was unkind to forbid and prohibit so great a satisfaction. This practice [they say] does not take the grace of God away from them, because all the same they go every day to church, and they do not believe that they have lost their place in Paradise; and even if they have to go to Hell, they believe and feel that at least they will already be familiar with the Devil, and the eternal torment, the flames of Hell and those of the Sabbath are the same thing. In addition, Satan does so many strange new things in this place, which their simplicity and credulity take for miracles, in such a way that when they are brought to judgement they do not weep nor shed a single tear, in fact their false martyrdom, be it torture or hanging, is so pleasing to them that many of them cannot wait to be executed, and joyfully suffer themselves to be brought to trial, so impatient are they to be with the Devil. And nothing in their imprisonment makes them so impatient as the fact that they cannot bear witness to him of how much they suffer and long to suffer for him, and they find it very strange that something so pleasant and agreeable should be punished or inquired into. The Devil himself gives them contentment and the comfort of leading them there while they are in prison.

Necato, a famous witch, superior and excelling all the others, from whom . . . nature had taken away her sex and made her into a man or a hermaphrodite . . . burnt and brown like a creature of the woods or a savage . . . bearded like a satyr . . . testified that when she was at the Sabbath, it was she, among others, who boiled the cauldron with the poisons, and skinned the snakes and toads; cutting off their heads with a knife she carried with her, and raising her fierce eyes to heaven, she said among other blasphemies . . . Ha, Philip, if I had you I would cut off your head as I do to these toads and snakes. Then, after striking the final blow, she threw them into the boiling cauldron in which these poisonous drugs were cooking.

Translation of the words accompanying the picture in the frontispiece (from de Lancre, Tableau de l'Inconstance . . . , 2nd edn)

A Satan is seated on a gilded throne, in the shape of a goat with five horns of which the fifth is alight, in order to light all the candles and fires of the Sabbath.

B The Queen of the Sabbath, crowned, on his right, and one less favoured on his left.

C Beneath his throne is a witch offering to him a child she has bewitched.

D Here are the guests at the assembly, each of whom has a demon beside him; and at this feast no other meat is served but carrion, the flesh of hanged men, the hearts of unbaptised children and other unclean beasts, quite outside the dealings and use of Christians, all insipid and without salt.

E These spectators are not admitted to the feast; they are poor witches thrust back into their corner, who dare not approach the great ceremonies.

F After the belly comes the dance [the French rhyme-joke (*pance — danse*) cannot be rendered in English], for when they are full up with meat, whether fleeting or illusory, or very harmful and disgusting, every demon leads the one who was beside him at table under this accursed tree, and there they dance; and the first has his face turned towards the centre of the ring, and the second outwards, and so on in the same way, and they dance and stamp and trip with the most indecent and filthy movements they can.

G These are the instrumentalists and the concert of music, to the singing and harmony of which they dance and leap.

H Below we see a troop of women and girls dancing, all with their faces turned away from the centre of the dance.

I Here is the cauldron on the fire, to make every kind of poison, whether to kill and bewitch men or to harm cattle, and one holds the snakes and toads in her hand, and the other cuts off their heads, and skins them, and throws them into the cauldron.

K During this business, more witches arrive at the Sabbath, on sticks and brooms, others on goats accompanied by children they have kidnapped and seduced, whom they come to offer to Satan. Others, leaving the Sabbath, carried through the air, are going to raise storms and tempests on the sea and elsewhere.

L These are the great lords and ladies, and other rich and powerful people, who deal with the big business of the Sabbath, where they appear veiled, and the women with masks, so as to remain always hidden and unrecognised.

M By this stream are the little children who, with white rods and switches, at a distance from the ceremonies, each guard the flocks of toads for those who usually bring them to the Sabbath.

The dance of the witches at the Sabbath, ibid., pp. 205ff.

The girls in Persia . . . worshipped the sun, dancing naked to the sound of some instrument, as do our witches, who dance at these accursed assemblies, sometimes naked and sometimes in their shift, with a big cat fastened to the back of it, as several of them have told us. . . .

They say that the dancers there always have their backs to the centre of the ring, and as a result the girls usually stretch their hands backwards in this round dance, dragging all the body backwards, and bending it over with the arms half turned round, so that most of them generally have large, swollen and prominent stomachs, rather pendulous at the front. I do not know whether this is caused by the dance or by the rubbish and bad food they are given to eat. For the rest, they dance very little one with one, that is to say a man alone with a woman or girl as we do in our galliards, but they told us and assured us that they only danced three sorts of branles, usually turning their shoulders one to the other, with everyone's back turned to the circle and their faces outwards. The first [branle] is of the gipsy type, because the wandering gipsies are half devils. . . .

The second [branle] is a leaping one such as our workpeople do in the towns and villages, through the streets and the fields; and these two are round dances. And the third is also done with the back turned, but in a longways set, and, without letting go of hands, they come so close to each other that they touch and meet back to back, a man with a woman; and at a certain cadence they collide and bump each other immodestly, buttocks to buttocks.

They dance to the sound of the little drum and the flute, and sometimes to that long instrument which they rest on the neck, then, extending it to about the waist, they strike it with a little stick; and sometimes to the violin. But these are not the only instruments of the Sabbath for we have learnt from several people that all sorts of instruments can be heard there, with such harmony that there is no concert in the world to equal it.

As for the lame, the cripples, the old wrecks and dodderers, they are the ones that dance the most lightly, for these are festivals of misrule, and everything seems out of order and against nature.

It is a remarkable thing that the very place, and the earth on which they trip and stamp their feet is visited with such a curse that neither grass nor anything else can grow on it. . . .

After the dance they sometimes begin to leap, and they go so far as to lay bets on who will execute the finest leap. . . .

Jeannette d'Abadie . . . tells us that the Devil sometimes watches the dances simply as a spectator, and sometimes leads the dance, often changing partners and seizing the hands of those who please him most. . . .

People describing those who dance in the French style say that the witches of Logny are wont to say while dancing: Har, Har, Devil, Devil, leap here, leap there, play here, play there; and the others said Sabbath, Sabbath, that is, festival and rest-day, to give a certain evidence of their joy, and that they are willing to serve and worship the Devil, and also to ape and imitate the Christians' worship of God. It is quite certain that the ancient Hebrews, taking their offerings to the temple, began to dance as soon as they approached the altar.

That the Devil in mockery of the most precious sacrament of the Church, has a kind of Mass celebrated at the Sabbath (ibid., pp. 457ff)

1 That the Devil shows himself seated at the Sabbath, and why.

The Devil, wishing to imitate Our Lord in everything, sits on a great gilded throne, magnificently decorated; just as Our Lord among his disciples was always seated, even when he was instructing his disciples in the temple: 'I sat daily with you teaching in the temple, and ye laid no hold on me' [Matth. 26: 55]. And Saint Augustine quotes the words in which our Lord says he 'taught seated, this belongs to the dignity of a master'. But Satan is mistaken, for he is seated at the Sabbath, and Jesus Christ is in church on the cross and not seated, and if he really wished to imitate him he would have had to let himself be crucified for his followers; and he would have to appear in that state in the said assemblies.

2 That the Devil exhibits, at the Sabbath, temples, altars, and demons on them in the form of saints.

So the Devil, wishing to ape and imitate the most holy works of God, shows himself seated, and causes temples to appear, and altars, and demons on them in the form of saints, music, bells, crosses; he has his Masters of Ceremonies, his prelates and bishops, his priests. But why do I say his priests? Has he not ours? He has three [kinds of] priests – the deacon, the subdeacon and the priest who says Mass, to imitate our High Mass. He uses candles, sprinkling and incense, and distributes it over the whole assembly. He has the sign of the cross on entering, the offertory, the sermon, the elevation and the *Ite Missa est*. Finally, he has the false martyrdom; and there are witches so ardent in his devilish service that no pain or torture can shake them, and you would say they were going to true martyrdom and death for love of him, as gaily as though they were going to a feast of delights and to a public celebration.

As for the Temple, certain girls who go to the Sabbath, who have often heard Mass said in their manner, have told us that they saw some sort of walls, like those of a church, with an altar set up, and on it a little demon the size of a child of twelve years who kept a smiling face and did not move, until this abominable mystery and trickery was finished, and when it was over the said altar and the statue vanished. The music is not only there when this Mass is said, but is always there as long as the said Sabbath lasts, and we are told that a vast number of instruments is heard, accompanied by a few little bells, so melodious that no one has ever heard such sweet harmony. . . . And on the said Sabbaths all these musicians and players of instruments cannot be seen, but only some little drummer after the fashion of the country. . . .

3 That the crosses and rosaries of the witches are always imperfect.

As for the crosses, they always wear them unbranched [i.e. with the crosspiece broken off], as we see them in cemeteries infected by the witches, in which the said Sabbaths are usually held. Spranger [author of *Malleus Maleficiarum* (Cologne, 1487)] observed and recorded that several witches had made a pact in so many words with Satan, to break the arms and the thighs of the crucifixes, even on Good Friday. . . .

It is the same with their rosaries which always have something odd about them. As examples, some witches of Ascain were once noticed who could not produce a rosary that was not defective, and who secretly wore in their bosoms wooden crosses newly made, as large as the ones that are put into the hands of those about to be executed; and sometimes all the beads were unequal in size, and badly strung, and in different colours, which shows that the Devil is constantly trying to vary, displace and change them.

4 [The] Bishop of the Sabbath.

There are bishops and prelates in the parish of St Pe itself. As the Devil had seen in the church the image of Saint Peter with a gilded tiara, the witnesses who were in the habit of going to the Sabbath told us that they had seen the young lord of Lancinena with a large hat made in the shape of this tiara; and he was commonly known and considered as the Bishop of the Sabbath. The Devil, while dancing, took him by the hand, and passing in front of him everyone saluted him as a person worthy of great respect. As for the priests, some of them were brought before us. . . . And they assured us that they had heard a form of High Mass being said, with deacon and subdeacon, and they were called by their name and surname. . . . Lighted candles are also seen, which they use in their worship and when they attend the false mysteries of this travesty of a mass; and they are made of resin, or, because this is not black enough, of pitch. . . .

5 Sprinkling and [the] sort of holy water at the Sabbath.

He also uses aspersion, and we have been assured that first the Devil urinates into a hole, and then all those at the Sabbath, great and small, and afterwards a man sometimes purposely throws it over the whole crowd, and sometimes the same water is seen in a hole made in the wall at the entrance of this miserable temple. As for the censer, I have not been able to note any peculiarity about it.

6 How the sign of the Cross is made at the Sabbath.

As for the sign of the Cross, if they want to mock us, they say:

In nomina Patrica, Aragueaco Petrica, Agora, Agora Valentia, Iouanda goure gaitz goustia.

Which means: *In the name of Patrice, Petrice of Aragon, at this hour Valencia, all our ills are over.*

On this subject we should note that there are three kinds of language in these few words, as the sign of the Cross is made in honour of the Trinity, which is what the Devil wants to mock. *In nomine Patrica*, these three first words are in Latin; *Aragueaco, Patrica, Agora, Agora, Valentia*, are in Spanish; *Iouanda, goure, gouaits, goustia*, are in Basque. And this sign of the Cross is made with the left hand, because Satan does everything the other way round from the Christians.

While making the sign of the cross they also use other filthy words, much more blasphemous than the others and without rhyme or reason except to deride the Mystery; and they say: *In nomine patrica, Aragueaco, Petrica, Gastellaco Ianicot, Equidac ipordian pot*. That means: In the name of Patrice, Petrice of Aragon, Jannicot of Castille, give me a kiss on my bottom.

7 The offertory taken at the Sabbath is of good silver.

During the service to Satan, and at the same time as they are worshipping him, they take the offertory in this way. Sometimes a man, sometimes a woman holds the basin into which the people at the Sabbath sometimes drop two crowns and sometimes one, of good silver (for it is not the Devil who is giving it), some more, some less, at their discretion and according to their means, for I have seen no rule about it . . . and the one collecting, and sometimes Satan himself, announces aloud and informs the assembly, that the money is for use at the trials which the witches have to face against those who are trying to condemn them to be burnt. . . .

8 [The] sermon preached at the Sabbath.

The Devil also preaches some sort of sermon in Basque, and he stands in a pulpit in the form of a goat, standing up on his hind legs, with his front legs on the pulpit, and other times it is one of the most famous witches, and this on Saturday evening. And we have been told that a man called Louis was seen preaching at Syboro, who instead of good instruction persuaded them to accuse the innocent and excuse the guilty, and always to bring many children to the Devil.

9 Monstrous Elevation of the Host at the Sabbath.

. . . Most people have always said . . . that some form of Mass was said at the Sabbath, the priest being dressed exactly like ours, and standing close to the Devil's side; and that the Elevation was done with a black host, quite simple, without anything engraved on it. . . .

That there is a sort of Elevation of a black host, not round, as they say, but made like a triangle. . . .

And an . . . inhabitant of Saint-Jean-de-Luz, aged fifteen years, stated that he had heard Mass said six or seven times at the Sabbath by Maître Jean Souhardibels, at the place called 'à la Cohandia', and he performed the Elevation, showing a black host, and he was raised up into the air, feet upwards and head downwards in front of the Devil, and he remained in that position during the Elevation, the time it would take to say a Credo. . . .

Jeanne d'Abadie says . . . that she has been taught at the Sabbath always to say at the Elevation of the chalice wherever it may be, and not at that of the sacred host: *Black raven, black raven*, being unable to utter any other prayer or to pronounce any other words but those ones, which she could not otherwise explain. The other witches say the same. . . .

And at the trial of the three priests of St-Jean-de-Luz . . . a witness accused one of these priests, among other things, of having said Mass, and done everything that priests customarily do; but with his face turned not towards the altar, but the other way round towards the congregation: and that after raising their host, as a sign of the greatest execration, he threw it down at once and trampled it underfoot.

10 When the witches call the Devil 'Barrabas'.

We have also noted several names which the witches give to the Devil their master when they are at the Sabbath; they call him Lord, Iauna, Master, the great master; but when they are in the hands of Justice, pretending to have a horror of him, to make the judges believe them, and to prove to them that they do not follow him at all, they call him contemptuously Barrabas, but sometimes they also call Our Lord Barrabas. . . .

11 That the Devil has introduced new Masses to the Sabbath, so as better to seduce all kinds of priests and monks.

The Devil is not content with this imitation; he wants a new kind of Mass to be said, with the result that the priests in Labourd indulge in feasting and debauchery to the very limit, which is very pleasant to the Devil, who does not in any way touch or destroy this holy and sacred Mystery.

Several people have told us that Maître Pierre Bocal, a priest, aged twenty-seven years, wanting to say the new Mass in the church of Siboro, tried two or three times at the Sabbath, the two or three preceding nights, whether he would perform the ceremonies well, and he said two or three Masses there, and the master of the nocturnal assembly and other small devils were on the altar in the form of small images of saints, and afterwards on the fourth day two new Masses were heard from him, one in the church of Siboro and the other at the Sabbath.

Unlike many medieval demonologists, who take everything they have heard in the trials as facts in the physical sense, de Lancre distinguishes between real things and those which depend on trickery and illusion. Yet no account is taken of statements put into the mouth of the accused by the inquisitors in the course of stereotyped interrogations usually accompanied by torture. However, we must emphasise once more that from the point of religious phenomenology we cannot make a distinction between the physically real and that which exists only in the imagination – of the accused, or even simply of the accusers – for both are manifestations of experiences which have in any case a psychological reality.

The general couriers of the Sabbath are the women, and its mysteries pass through their hands [rather] than through those of the men. The facts expressed in this sentence are extremely important, and if we are to explain and confirm them in more detail we must dig a little deeper.

The religious and cultural background of Christianity ensured from the very beginning that it must at least partially reject anything to do with the 'eternal feminine'. This rejection applied on the one hand to the elemental and earthy aspect of the cult, with its many references to fertility and sexuality, and on the other hand to the devouring, fearful aspect of the female, which Erich Neumann calls 'the negative elemental character'.[54] It is true that until the early Middle Ages the figure of Mary still had some essential features of the image of totality implied by the 'Great Mother'.[55] However, in the course of the Middle Ages, partly due to the influence of the troubadours, Mary became a one-sided image of light and purity. The 'beloved Lady' of so many songs has practically nothing left of the fullness and strength of the old mother-goddesses. It was, indeed, in the Middle Ages that Mary was also considered as a cosmic symbol,[56] but this symbolism evolved on a high spiritual plane and transcended the earth in its magical and concrete aspects. In the Christian religion women played a part only in the early days, as prophetesses and deaconesses, and when Christianity became a state religion women were deprived of any real liturgical function.[57] At the same time, medieval theologians were setting a lower and lower value on women – an attitude quite foreign to that of the early Church[58]. The witches' sabbath is a powerful reaction against the repression of women in the Christian world.

In his study *Erdmutter und Hexe*[59] Anton Mayer seeks out the connections between the ancient worship of the Earth-Mother and the medieval witch cult. The tradition of earth worship, to which earth magic, sorceresses and prophetesses, the cult of trees and groves and many other things belong, had its roots in a general Indo-Germanic or even pre-Indo-Germanic culture and was then concentrated in two centres, the Mediterranean and the Nordic. 'The southern and northern branches developed side by side until they overlapped, first when classical antiquity in its Roman form came into contact with the Germanic world and during the great migrations, and then during the spread of Christianity.'[60] Thus, in the female cult of the witches' sabbath classical elements mingled with elements of the Nordic, and particularly Germanic, tradition.

Will-Erich Peuckert[61] has drawn our attention to an essential difference between the southern and the northern types of witch cult. The Mediterranean witches and their forerunners appear mostly in groups, while the northern witch was originally a solitary being, so that very few Nordic sagas – such as the Blocksberg saga with its variants[62] – mention the witches' coven. At the same time the northern tradition of the witches' sabbath, despite the influence of the southern tradition of the Satan cult proper, which always implies a community, offers very little material in comparison with the Romance tradition. Later, too, the Romance-speaking countries produced far more examples of the black mass than those of the north. That is why we have almost entirely given up the idea of quoting texts from the latter region, as we are anxious to choose the most informative documents possible. The less useful sources can quite easily be placed in the contexts indicated in our account.

The Great Mother appears above all in the form of the 'Queen of the Sabbath', whom we met first in the Old Spanish text. She is magnificently adorned and sits on Satan's right (see frontispiece, reference B). The Queen of the Sabbath is a sort of antitype to the Queen of Heaven, the crowned Virgin Mary; she embodies some of the spirit of the Near-Eastern, classical and Germanic mother goddesses of the earth and the underworld (Ishtar, Cybele, Isis, Gaia, Hecate, Artemis-Diana,[63] Baubo, Persephone, Hel, Freya, Nerthus, and so on). Satan and the Queen of the Sabbath form the 'divine couple' under whose aegis the nightly celebration takes place.

In his work *La Sorcière*,[64] which first appeared in 1862, Jules Michelet made a reconstruction of the sabbath ritual in which he attributed detailed functions to the priestess corresponding to the Queen of the Sabbath. Her body is said to have served as a 'living altar' but I have found no support for this in the sources, although it influenced some later publications on the black mass, particularly French ones. As far as I know the body of a woman was not used as an altar for the black mass before the second half of the seventeenth century.

In the early Middle Ages the idea of witches' flight was still considered pure fantasy. The so-called *Canon Episcopi* (*c.* 900) describes women who fly through the night as *daemonum illusionibus et phantasmatibus seductae* – seduced by illusions and fantasies of the demons.[65] But in the following centuries the belief in the physical reality of the phenomenon generally took root, and de Lancre is convinced of it. There are many pictures of the flight (see frontispiece, reference K). Brooms and sticks, phallic symbols, are an analogy in a diabolised form of the Thyrus wands of the maenads in Ancient Greece. The experience of flight, as Mircea Eliade shows in his article 'Der magische Flug',[66] is closely connected with ecstasy; man breaks the fetters of his everyday existence and rises into the realms of the superhuman. The motif of flight also has connections with the Dionysian cult.[67] In their ecstatic flight the female followers of Satan (who, as the text says, often personally carries the witches through the air) are taken out of their everyday existence and transported to the place of Satanic worship.

The text gives, as the forms assumed by the Devil, a goat (which we have already mentioned), a tree-trunk, and a dark man of monstrous size. The tree, following the classical and Germanic vegetation cult, very often appears in witchcraft,[68] and has been since primitive times the favourite home for divine spirits (see for example the Donarseiche at Geismar in Hessen, felled by Boniface). If, as here, the trunk is emphasised, the phallic aspect of the tree comes to the fore[69]. As a man, Satan, according to de Lancre, is 'tortured, agonised' – a similar characterisation to that in the Spanish source.

In almost all descriptions and pictures of the sabbath, a large cauldron, in which all kinds of gruesome flesh is cooked to make poison, takes an important place (see frontispiece, reference I). Demonologists are constantly listing the revolting ingredients of the cauldron. It cannot be determined how much of this is exaggeration and fantasy, nor – especially – to what extent children were killed and their flesh cooked. These children had to be unbaptised, because in this way they could not go to Heaven and increase the kingdom of God. The use of toads and snakes gave the poison its chthonic power (we are not considering the chemical and toxological point of view; this would have to be tested with regard to the products of the decomposition of protein). Knowledge about the healing and harmful materials derived from plants and animals, and about medicines and poisons, has from earliest times been the domain of women.[70] The witches, corresponding to their opposite function in Christianity, use only the negative side of this ancient knowledge.

The food eaten at the witches' feast (see frontispiece, reference D) is put together in the same way as the contents of the cauldron. The character of this perverted Agape-feast is cannibalistic, or, as psychoanalysis would say, oral-aggressive.

The witches' feast is a parallel to the embryo-communion of the Phibionites (see above, p. 25ff). Here too the participants identify

The Sabbath Meal of the Witches. *(Michelet)*

with the destructive and devouring aspect of the Great Mother, which Christianity did not accept. In order to gain a deeper understanding of this process, we may give a longer quotation from Eric Neumann, who has clearly explained the ambivalence of the female element:

> Witches and vampires, ghouls and spectres from the myths and legends of every race, period and country have a terrifying similarity to our own nightmares. . . . For us, world, life, nature and soul are female-bearing and nourishing, protecting and warning. But the female image has its reverse side, and humanity sees death and disaster, danger and want, hunger and helplessness as abandonment to the dark and terrible mother. The bosom of the earth becomes the death-dealing gnashing jaws of the underworld and beside the earth's fruitful womb and the mountain's protecting hollows gape Hell and the abyss, the dark, deep hole, the devouring maw of the grave, darkness and nothingness. For this woman, who brings forth life and everything living upon earth, devours it all again, hunts down her quarry and captures it with snares and nets. . . . Everywhere . . . where the female appears in her terrifying aspect, she is also the primeval snake-woman, the woman with a phallus. . . . That is why the Gorgon is given all the male attributes – the serpent, the tooth, the boar's tusk, the protruding tongue,

> and sometimes even a beard. . . . The fertility ritual of the Great Mother includes blood-sacrifice and dismemberment, both of which fertilise the earth's womb. This is still alive in a number of rites in which the fragments of the sacrifice – man or beast – are ceremoniously spread over the fields. The Greek Thesmophoria, in which piglets, the symbolic children of the Earth-sow and phallic symbols, were thrown into a hole in the earth said to be infested with snakes, belongs in this context. . . . The decomposed remains of the sacrifice were later brought out of the hole and spread over the earth as fertility magic. It was thought necessary to achieve fertility and resurrection for the earth and for life – thought of as feminine – through blood, death and corpses; this conception, constantly strengthened by the alternation of life and death in nature, gives the Earth Mother a terrifying, destroying and death-dealing image.[71]

The maenads in particular illustrate the double nature of women. They are motherly beings, fostering young deer and wolves, and at the same time madwomen who tear men and beasts to pieces[72] (see the stories of the children of Argus, Pentheus and Orpheus). In the *Bacchae* of Euripides the herdsman reports to Pentheus:

> *O, then we fled, and fleeing scantly scaped*
> *The Bacchanals' rending grasp. Down swooped they then*
> *Upon our pasturing kine with swordless hand.*
> *Then hadst thou seen thy mother in her grip*
> *Clutch a deep-uddered heifer bellowing loud;*
> *And others rent the calves in crimson shreds.*
> *Ribs hadst thou seen and cloven hoofs far hurled*
> *This way and that, and flakes of flesh that hung*
> *And dripped all blood bedabbled 'neath the pines.*
> *Bulls, chafing, lowering fiercely along the horn*
> *Erewhile, were tripped and hurled unto the earth.*
> *Dragged down by countless-clutching maiden hands.*
> *More swiftly was the flesh that lapped their bones*
> *Stripped, than thou couldst have closed thy kingly eyes.*[73]

As a child of the Titans, Dionysus himself, according to the Orphic tradition, was cut into pieces and thrown into a boiling cauldron. The primitive story says that his limbs – including the heart and the phallus – were then burnt, and the vine grew from the ashes. The death of the god is symbolised in the Dionysian cult by the sacrifice of a calf, a kid, or other animals.[74] In the north, the Wild Hunt[75] corresponds to a certain extent to the fury of the maenads. It was led not only by Odin (Wotan) in the guise of a storm-god, but also, in some traditions, by women (Wode, Gode, Diana, Herodias and so on). The Valkyries,[76] who do the will of Odin, also have similarities with the maenads. Odin himself, the restless wanderer, was destined to die like Dionysus; he was run through with a spear and hung on the Tree of Life:

> *I know that I hung on the windy tree*
> *Nine long nights,*
> *Wounded by the spear, sacrificed to Odin,*
> *I myself to myself . . .*[77]

These parallels raise a series of problems the nucleus of which can best be demonstrated by reference to the short extract in which de Lancre talks about the seated position of the Devil at the sabbath (see p. 70). De Lancre compares the seated Devil with the crucified Christ, and adds: 'if he really wished to imitate him, he would have had to let himself be crucified for his followers'. What does this mean?

From the psychological point of view the negative character of the female element represents the unconscious, insofar as it threatens and devours the conscious mind. From the point of view of religious phenomenology it is the subhuman and the superhuman element destroying what is limited and earthly. The destructiveness of the Great Female can only be overcome by an act of sacrifice; and this is the act at which the negative, female element aims. 'It is a part of the mysteries of the Great Goddess and the essence of her spiritual character that she achieves life only through death, and development only through suffering. As ruler of men and beasts she will permit no birth and life without suffering.'[78] This mystery is expressed in Christ's death on the mother-tree, the tree of the cross,[79] and his resurrection; in the dismembered Dionysus boiled in the cauldron and resurrected as the vine; in the wounded Odin hung on the mother-tree and his rescue by the magic power of the runes;[80] in innumerable other myths and in all corresponding religions (cf. the fertility rites of the Thesmophoria, mentioned earlier). This is the source of the tragic aspect of Satan and the Satan cult, not only of the witches' sabbath.

Satan knows no death and resurrection, he has no part in the mysteries of death and rebirth. This, in fact, is the reason why he is sad, tormented, hectic and destructive – all signs of sterile, false suffering instead of true fateful suffering, the only kind that leads to transformation and new life. It is a genuine tragic situation. Satan, God's adversary, represents the dark side of the divinity, which has, as it were, split off from the rest. But for that very reason the mystery of the suffering son of God is closed to him. In the conditions of traditional Christianity there is no way out; if Satan were to submit himself to the cross he would have to give up his role as adversary, and the perfect whole of the divinity would be lost. Even a return to a pre-Christian status – such as that of Dionysus – is denied him, for the Christian position is an extreme one and demands a corresponding extreme to stand against it. De Lancre's statement is true, but his 'challenge' to Satan to imitate Christ in his crucifixion cannot be fulfilled. As de Lancre says, 'Satan is mistaken'; the self-deception in his avoidance of the cross is the essence of his whole existence. It is an unavoidable deception for the sake of truth, a lie that truth demands just as much as it condemns. Christ suffered 'without the gate' (Heb. 13: 12); and in the *Mysterium iniquitatis*, the 'mystery of evil' this 'without the gate' has an almost immeasurable poignancy.

As the maenads and the other followers of Dionysus participate in his nature, so do those assembled at the sabbath have their part in the nature of Satan. The witches, male and female, are excluded from the mystery of rebirth, and this is the cause of their one-sided destructiveness and sterility. It is significant that de Lancre says that the place where the witches dance is so accursed that nothing more can grow on it, and that the seed of men at the sabbath, though it is normal sperm, cannot beget children any more than the seed of Satan himself. This too expresses the tragedy of the Satan cult: it is the revival of pre-Christian fertility rites, yet it is condemned to infertility.

Unlike Satan, the witches have the chance to experience the *Mysterium crucis*, the 'mystery of the Cross', itself. There are passages telling us how so many witches longed to suffer for the Devil (see for example p. 66), how they could hardly wait to be

The Burning of Witches. *(Woodcut, 1555)*

tortured and executed, and went to their deaths with joyful hearts, in the firm belief that they would be finally united with Satan. These reports resemble the stories of the death of the martyrs, and in fact de Lancre speaks of a 'false martyrdom'. Even this martyrdom has its tragic aspect; Satan, for whom the women go joyfully to their deaths, will never be united with them; even death is denied to him. The bridegroom in the marriage of death exists only in the imagination. In their self-immolation the witches leave their master behind, and even the 'good God' is no longer present. The dying witch is utterly homeless. The 'false martyrdom' can come to fruition only on a plane beyond traditional Christian dualism.

Satan receives from those taking part in the sabbath a ritual kiss on the buttocks – the Spanish source gives a vivid picture of this (see p. 55). In the Christian body symbolism which developed in the Middle Ages, the buttocks, like the genital area, were considered as the zone of darkness, Hell and the Devil, while the spiritual and the divine were connected with the upper part of the body and its organs. This symbolism has affected Catholic moral theology up to our own time, through the division of the body into *partes honestae*, *minus honestae* and *inhonestae* – honourable, less honourable and dishonourable parts.[81] It is here that the dualistic Christian conception is most clearly expressed, in contrast to that of the Greeks, who gave Aphrodite the nickname 'Kallipygos', 'she of the beautiful buttocks'. The Christian conception of the posterior area is connected with the taboo on the dark primeval Great Female. The example of the well-known 'Venus of Willendorf', which dates from palaeolithic times, shows that the posterior parts of prehistoric goddesses were notably broad and full; their 'firm seat' upon the earth is obvious.[82] (From the psychoanalytical point of view this is the taboo on anal-pregenital sexuality.) Through the kiss on the buttocks the witches bind themselves in a unique way to Satan's chthonic nature. Joseph von Görres in his *Christliche Mystik* expresses this as follows: 'It is characteristic for the goat-form of the evil spirit to be given a second face, looking downwards, a thing of darkness, closely connected with the organs of excretion, which all face downwards. . . . The kiss is pressed upon the centre of this face, and the one who kisses binds himself to eternal servitude under the absolute rule of evil.'[83]

We come now to the sexual orgies of the sabbath. We cannot discuss this subject without reference to the psychopathological aspect. So, with regard to what we have already seen on p. 18ff., we must first make some observations on the connection between the phenomenological and the psychological or psychopathological view of the sabbath orgies.

From the latter point of view we find every possible perversion – incest, homosexuality, sadism, masochism, and so on. It is emphasised that they provide 'marvellous pleasure', and the Spanish source describes a woman after copulation with Satan as 'very proud and satisfied'. It might appear best to accept the psychoanalytical explanation, according to which these perversions show a regression to infantile pregenital phases of sexual development[84] in revolt against Christian sexual morality, which is strictly genital and monogamous. (The sociological problems arising in this connection – to mention only the key words matriarchy and patriarchy, and the Oedipus complex as origin or effect of a culture[85] – cannot be discussed here.) Such an explanation has all the more to recommend it since previous interpretations of the orgies within the Satan cult or its fringe phenomena (see pp. 29, 47) do not apply to the sabbath, because in this case the orgies have no obvious 'pneumatic' or 'ecstatic' character, but pleasure is rather sought for its own sake. A further possibility that has been considered hinges on the psychology of the collective unconscious. According to this, abnormal modes of behaviour are to be related to their archetypal symbolic content. Incest is a return to a primitive state in which the conscious mind is identified with the collective unconscious represented by the Great Mother,[86] homosexuality expresses an identification with the archetype of the hermaphrodite, the primeval androgyne,[87] and so on. We have always taken the last-named point of view when the justification came from the phenomenon itself, that is to say when the symbolic reference to the archetypal background (which, however, we always regard as something trans-psychic and cosmic) was inherent in the subject under consideration as such. There is no doubt that the sabbath orgies have not only an individual psychological significance, but an archetypal one as well. But the phenomenon would be diminished to an inadmissable degree if we considered it exclusively in the light of these two aspects.

Those examined by de Lancre, referring to their sexual experiences at the sabbath, speak of 'contentment', 'joy', 'an agreeable and pleasant thing'. A passage we have not quoted speaks of 'a wonderful sensual delight' and the fact that afterwards the women feel 'complete fulfilment'.[88] These expressions denote a sexual experience beyond personal feeling or symbolic definition – a direct possession by what Georg Groddeck calls the *Es* or *Id* (Freud took this idea over, but limited it to the individual unconscious.)[89] The pure id is pre-archetypal; 'the symbolism that accompanies all relationships in life' is a 'form of the id'.[90] Thus the Great Female is a form of the id, and not the other way round. Naturally the id is also pre-conscious, and the more submerged in it a person becomes, the more involved he is with the unconscious. The 'way to the id' leads first of all back to early childhood, and this is what lends early forms of sexuality – going beyond psychoanalytical theories – such great fascination for adults. They are more 'permeable' for the id than standardised forms of 'mature' sexuality, which are near to the conscious mind and more or less spiritualised.[91] The way leads further back, as the sabbath itself shows, to the animal level; the witches believe that they are sometimes turned into animals or they play the role of a 'succubus'.[92]

The sabbath orgy is not a means of ecstatic liberation from the

Woman with an Incubus.

fetters of the body, but rather the contrary: a descent to the physical and animal level, there to become a part of the great, pleasure-giving and yet painful force which has been largely repressed or sublimated in Christian cultures. But it would be wrong to project ideas from modern sexual mystique[93] into the orgies of the witches' sabbath, for they rest on quite different premises, born of the intellectualism and subjectivism of modern man.

The witch Necato tells of a rite which corresponds to some extent with the *fractio panis* – breaking of bread – in the Christian mass. The heads of snakes and toads are cut off with the following words: 'Ha, Philip, if I had you, I would cut off your head as well.' In a long explanation (which we do not print as it is scarcely credible) de Lancre connects the name Philip with the legend of the Apostle Philip.[94] Michelet[95] believes the curse contains a memory of King Philip of Valois (1328–50), under whom the Hundred Years' War between France and England had begun; after the French defeat at Crécy (1346) the people endured terrible sufferings through famine and heavy taxation, leading later to peasant risings which were suppressed with much bloodshed. Henry T. F. Rhodes[96] also considers King Philip the Fair (1285–1314). In any case we may assume that this curse provided an outlet for the hate of the lower orders against a

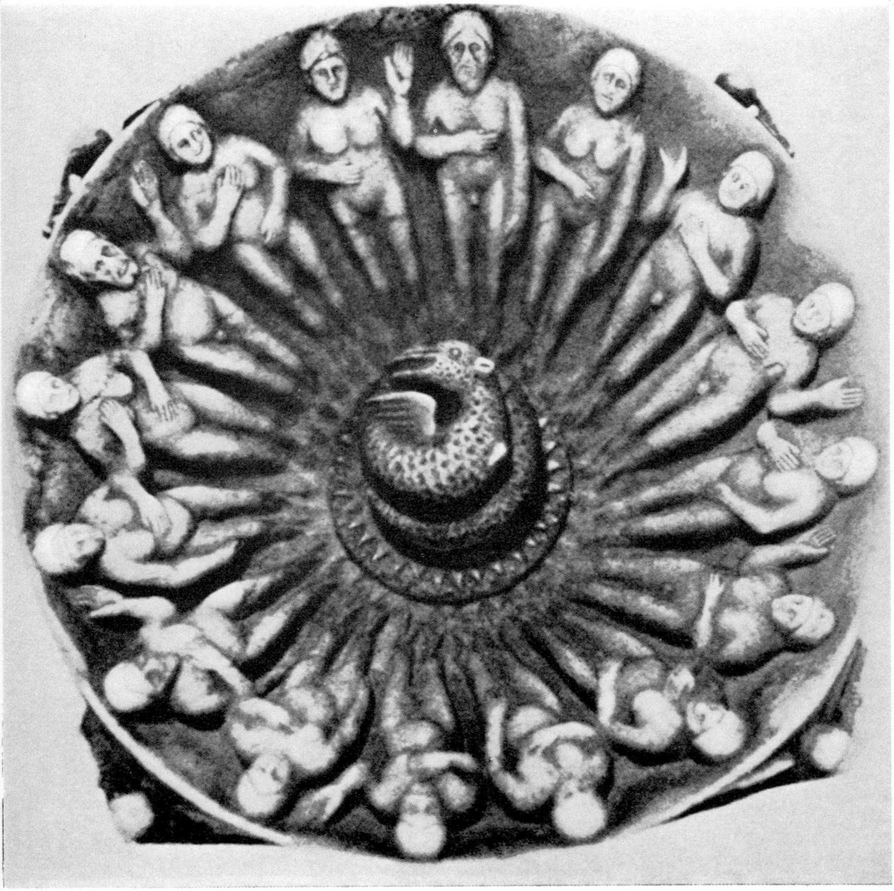

Snake Worship: alabaster bowl from the region of the Hellenistic mysteries, private collection, Paris; from *Eranos Jahrbuch VII (1939)* (Rhein-Verlag, Zurich, 1940)

Abbé Guibourg celebrates black mass for Madame de Montespan: engraving by Henry de Valvost for Jules Bois, *Le Satanisme et la Magie* (Paris, 1903)

symbol of oppression. The sociological interpretation of the witches' sabbath comes in here. Considering the large number of people attending (the sources naturally exaggerate this, sometimes immoderately), the character of the sabbath as an expression of the people's revolt against the ruling classes becomes extremely important. More detailed study of this theme must be left to sociologists and historians.

The dance at the sabbath (see frontispiece, references F and H) is erotic and sexual in character, and so belongs to the orgy; but at the same time it is connected with the fertility dances that exist all over the world, and are attested as far back as the Old Stone Age.

Women Dancing. *(Palaeolithic rock painting from Cogul)*

For instance, women are dancing around a naked man with an exaggeratedly large phallus,[97] with their feet they are bringing the earth fertility – *mana* – personified in the phallic figure. The sabbath dance shows clear parallels to dances of this kind, but, as we have said, it is destined to be sterile.

De Lancre says that *branles* are danced at the sabbath. The branle (from the French *branler* – to stagger, sway) is usually a longways dance, the chief characteristic of which is the 'chain-like meeting and outward movement of the dancing couples'.[98] The lines of dancers are therefore in constant motion backwards and forwards. The branle is of definitely popular origin and often contains elements of pantomime; many forms are danced (generally as a suite) which is why the text speaks of 'only' three kinds. Although the branle has the medieval longways form, it is one of the dances of the Renaissance period. So at the witches' sabbath, which belongs essentially to the late Middle Ages, we come up against an element of a more modern epoch. The 'françoise', which is also danced, is, unlike the branle, a processional dance in which men and women dance independently.[99]

The details of the black mass described by de Lancre, which he calls an 'abominable mystery and buffoonery', need only a few short explanations, since the author himself gives a commentary. Indubitably priests of the Church did celebrate such masses; this is important because, according to a Catholic belief not challenged by the sabbath community, a priest who is living in mortal sin or has forsaken the Church still retains the power to consecrate. It is also important that at that time the black mass was beginning to penetrate into the church buildings themselves. Many details that emerge give the impression that they are supplied for the sake of completeness in the reversal of ecclesiastical institutions and customs (this applies for example to the exact specification of Satan's clerical hierarchy). The levitation of the priest and his turning around in the air may be a definite hallucination, but the fact that he faces the congregation instead of the altar recalls the early Church, in which this position – though behind, not in front of the altar – was customary. The precise meaning of the words spoken when making the sign of the cross is obscure. The words 'black raven' spoken at the Elevation, are connected with animal symbolism.[100] In classical mythology the raven, originally white, was the symbol of Apollo, Helios and Mithras, a messenger of the gods and a bird of prophecy. For the Germanic peoples, because of its aggressive nature and its preference for flesh, even that of corpses, it was the bird of the war-god Wotan. For Christians, because of its black colour, it became predominantly an image of impurity, darkness and sin, and thus a bird of the Devil, and also – as in Gen. 8: 6f. – a symbol of the apostates and heretics who left the Ark of the Church and did not return. The invocation 'black raven' may be either a blasphemy against Christ, present through the consecration, or an identification of the divine presence, achieved by consecration, with Satan. Here we touch upon a problem which is to be discussed as part of the interpretation of the following source:

3 Quite a different spirit is evident in the passages taken from a work which appeared about a decade after that of de Lancre.

Histoire véritable et mémorable de ce qui c'est passé sous l'exorcisme de trois filles possédées és pais de Flandre, en la découverte et confession de Marie de Sains . . . et Simone Dourlet complice, et autres, etc. Extraict des memoires de Messire Nicolas de Momorenci . . . et du R.P.F. Sebastien Michaëlis [O.P.] . . . et du R.P.F. François Donsieux . . ., mis en lumiere par J. le Normant . . . etc., Première partie, Paris 1623

Treatise I
Sins committed in the Synagogue Chapter IV, pp. 32f.

Speaking, then, of the sabbath held on 24 May 1613, she [Marie de Sains] said they had held up proceedings at a council meeting that day, that they had taken a sacred host after the celebration of Mass and put it on a table and that all those concerned with the Sabbath gathered round it and each said whatever blasphemies he wished against the sacred Host. She said that every Friday they take the image of Christ crucified and hurl mockery of the Passion at it, whip it, deal cuffs at it, spit in its face, strike on the crown of thorns, pull out the nails from hands and feet and put them back, open the side to renew the wounds and hurts, and on the feet, hands and side they put a consecrated Host so that it may receive the blows and insults.

She also said and declared that this time [i.e. on the sabbath in question] they did not take a wooden or alabaster crucifix, but one made of bread, which they later consecrated; she said they had first dishonoured it in a thousand ways, and that afterwards they trampled it underfoot and hacked it to pieces, which they threw to the dogs to eat. She said, moreover, that on that same night she took a sacred host and put it in dirty places, declaring that she had consumed the sacred host, pressing and pulverising it between her fingers, and several others had done the same thing . . . and at the same time some people had burnt the sacred host, and others had cut it into pieces, and others had boiled it.

Treatise II
The worship which those at the Sabbath render to the Devil, Chapter II, ibid., p. 56

. . . She said that every Sunday the blood of Our Lord is thrown on those who are present, and they all cry in Latin: 'His blood be upon us and upon our children' [Matth. 27: 25], and that this was done instead of holy water to ape the Church. . . . During the sacrifice they commit a thousand indignities; some put out their tongues, others blaspheme, others expose their private parts, and the greatest of the Synagogue commit the greatest indignities. At the Elevation the devils go to the altar and turn their backsides towards the holy Sacrament, and the sorcerers and sorceresses, and the leaders of the Synagogue do the same thing as the devils. . . . Instead of the *Ite Missa est* they say 'Go to all the devils' . . .

(Example of a sermon on the Sabbath), ibid., p. 69

My friends, today we celebrate the sabbath of sodomy. Sodomy is a work very pleasant to Lucifer. I beg you to do your duty well; indeed, that you should all incite each other. Take example from me who am the prince of lechery, and if you accomplish this work often, you will have your reward in this world, and in the other, eternal life.

If we compare this source with the preceding one, we notice considerable differences. In the first place – and this holds good for the whole work from which the extracts are taken – it is almost entirely the purely negative side of the Satan cult that has survived. In the second place, the sabbath ritual is paralleled almost mechanically with the offices of the Church. The *Histoire veritable* . . . contains, for example, Satanic versions of the Paternoster, the Ave Maria, the Credo and the Litany, as well as a whole collection of sermons by the Devil for the Church festivals of the year. This is systematised in various ways; special blasphemies and sexual perversions are ordained for the different days of the week.[101] Since the passages in question are somewhat dull, we give only one short extract from a sermon as a characteristic example.

In the first two passages the spiritual attitudes of the late Middle Ages are mingled with baroque elements. We come up against a perversion of the specific mystique of wounds and suffering that developed in the baroque era.

If consecrated hosts are beaten, dishonoured in various ways and destroyed, this indicates that the presence of Christ in them is understood in an absolutely concrete and realistic way. For the Satanists as we see them in this document, the act of consecration is of primary importance to their practices, as it enables them to have the hated Christ literally in their hands. At this point we must look back.

De Lancre's reports too show that the Satanists are convinced of the reality of consecration, and he too says that the host was cursed, flung to the ground and trampled upon. However the invocation 'black raven' at the Elevation has led some people to wonder whether there is not an identification of Christ with Satan. The question is all the more apposite because the host is black, the Devil's own colour.[102] We can only guess at the answer. First of all comes the Elevation – the contrary of the act of throwing it on the ground – and everyone, under an almost magical compulsion, as a woman says (see p. 74), speaks the 'prayer' in question, but then the host is dishonoured and trampled upon; this shows that something between the two modes of behaviour has taken place. Perhaps we can conclude that there has been a kind of disappointment that the attempt at identification has not succeeded. The black host cannot wipe out the memory of the white host, Christian ideas are constantly forcing their way into the anti-Christian cult, and curses and destruction cannot but follow. The Satanists have not succeeded in imitating the liturgy of the Church; the attempt to become master of the mystery itself fails, and this is obvious immediately after the consecration. This failure hangs together with what we have said about Satan's exclusion from the mystery of death and resurrection. The liturgy of the mass is essentially an actualising and renewing of the Crucifixion, so that the identification of Satan with Christ, who is literally present, or the supplanting of Christ by Satan are equally unattainable.

D *Gilles de Rais*

A work on the Satan cult must of necessity include a late medieval figure in which the destructive aspect of Satanism is concentrated in an extreme form. This figure is Gilles de Rais;[103] and he must be mentioned even though the sources concerning him do not tell us of any extensive rites of devil worship (which is why we have not reproduced any long passages from them) and although his actions must largely be seen from a purely psychopathological point of view.

Gilles de Rais was born in 1404 of a noble family. He lost his father at the age of eleven and was brought up by his weak grandfather, Jean de Craon. He grew up undisciplined and immoderately ambitious. His estates made him the leading member of the Breton nobility, and he became through marriage one of the richest men in France. Not only did he distinguish himself in several military campaigns, he was also extremely cultured and interested in books, music and the theatre. He then became the constant companion and bodyguard of Joan of Arc. On the occasion of the Coronation in Rheims (1429) he was raised to the rank of Marshal of France, although only twenty-five years old. But four years later he retired to his estates and began a life of luxury and debauchery. At the same time he occupied himself with alchemy, and for his experiments, which had, of course, to include the evocation of demons, he brought in a number of sorcerers, including the Italian Francesco Prelati. In the chambers and vaults of his castles, such as the crypt of Tiffauges, he murdered, according to the records of his trial, about a hundred and forty children over the years, in order to sacrifice them to Satan or some demon, or simply to satisfy his sadistic lusts. The children were enticed in, kidnapped or bought. As the sources say 'He sat on their bellies and took immense pleasure in seeing them die thus, and laughed over it,[104] and 'He took more pleasure in killing them, and watching them droop and die, and seeing their blood, than in lechery with them'.[105] In J. K. Huysmans's book *Là-bas*[106] there are detailed descriptions of Gilles de Rais's sadistic practices, which do not, however, appear in the source documents. Gilles de Rais had aroused the enmity of influential nobles, and this led to his being brought before both ecclesiastical and secular courts. It is not certain whether his self-accusations and tearful protestations of repentance before death were genuine or mere exhibitionism. On 26 October 1440, he was hanged, together with his servants, amid the sympathy of a crowd whose attitude had been completely reversed by his confession of guilt and plea for forgiveness. Gilles de Rais has repeatedly been compared with Bluebeard, and may even have been the origin of this legendary figure, known to the world through Charles Perrault.

Huysmans has an interesting explanation of the figure of Gilles de Rais:

> This man was . . . a true mystic . . . His association with Joan of Arc certainly sharpened his ardent impulse towards God. From exalted mysticism to bitter satanism is but a step. There are no sharp dividing lines in that realm beyond reality. He lavished on the service of evil all the fervour he brought to his prayers. . . . It can be a matter of pride to be as great in crime as a saint in virtue – and that is the essence of Gilles de Rais.[107]

Exaggerated though this interpretation may be, it certainly has a nucleus of truth.

E *The secret initiation rites of the Templars*

Among the darkest elements of the Satanic tradition are the blasphemous initiation rites of the Templars. They form the most substantial part of the prosecution's case in the seven-year-long trial which led in 1312 to the dissolution of the order by Pope Clement V, and ended in 1314 with the burning of the Grand Master Jacques de Molay, Geoffroy de Charnay, preceptor of Normandy, and other knights.[108] The liquidation of the Templars was the work of Philip the Fair. The great power of the order, founded in 1119, was a thorn in the king's flesh; but above all he was eager to acquire the Templars' property, as his financial situation at the time was desperate.

The hearings were carried out to a rigid pattern, involving up to 127 questions. Here are some extracts from the very full records:

Le Procès des Templiers. From the examination of Huguet de Bure (24 April 1310) (Michelet, I, pp. 205ff)

. . . asked how long he had been in the said order of the Temple, and where, by whom and how he had been admitted, he replied that prior to their arrest he had been three years in the order and had been admitted in a house of the order called Fontanette, in the diocese of Langres, by Brother P. de Bure, a brother acting as preceptor in this house, who was, he said, now dead. He added that the said Brother P., who received him in a certain chapel in the said house, when the witness had taken off all the clothes he was wearing, except his shirt and breeches, gave him the robes and mantle of the order, and at once kissed the witness, first on the mouth, secondly on the navel, and thirdly on the backbone, above the place where the belt is fastened; he said this same Brother P. lifted the witness's clothes before and behind, when, as mentioned, he kissed him on the navel and on the backbone.

He also said that immediately after the foregoing, Brother P. brought a cross, and ordered the witness to spit on the cross and trample on it with his feet and renounce Jesus three times. And when the witness wondered at the kisses on his navel and his backbone, and at such orders, and said he was unwilling to do what the said Brother P. ordered, Brother P. said he must do the above-mentioned things because it was part of the rules of the order of the Temple, and if he did not do these things, he well knew what they would do to him. And then Brother Guillaume de Bure, a priest of the said order, a blood brother of this witness, now dead, who, he said, was present at this initiation, and no other, told the witness that he should do the above-mentioned things, and when he heard this, the witness denied Jesus three times, as he said, with his lips but not his heart, and spat once on the cross, but did not trample it underfoot.

He also said that immediately after the foregoing, the said Brother P. took a head out of a cupboard in the chapel and put it on the altar; then he put a cord round the said head, and giving the cord to the witness, told him to keep it constantly tied round over his shirt; but he said he did not wear it. . . .

Asked with what words he denied Jesus, he replied that it was with these words: *I deny God, I deny God, I deny God*. Asked whether all these things were done in the same place, he replied yes, and in the same chapel, in front of the altar, after dawn, without removal to another place. Asked whether there were any lights then in the said chapel, he answered no; but he could see clearly because day was breaking, so that he could easily distinguish the said cross.

Asked what the said cross was made of, he said of wood, and it was painted with the image of Christ crucified, about half a cubit in size. Asked what the head was like, he replied that it was not of wood, but appeared to be of silver, or copper, or gold; and it was exactly like a human head, with a face, and a long beard, almost white. Asked whose the said head was, he replied that he did not know, and that he never saw the said head again, because, he said, he had not been more than two days in the house since then, and the said preceptor, after the said initiation, put the head back into the said cupboard.

Asked what the said cord was like, he replied that it was of fine white thread and of a length that could be tied round the body. Asked why he did not wear the said cord, since he had done other more serious things he had been told to do, he replied that he thought it a sin, because he had seen it tied around that head, and he did not believe the head had any good meaning. . . . Asked how many years it was since he entered the said order, he replied twenty-seven years or thereabouts.

From the interrogation of Jacques de Troyes (9.V.1310). (ibid., pp. 255ff)

He said that the man who initiated him [Radulphus de Gisiaco] stripped him completely naked in the presence of the other brothers who were looking on, and told him to kiss his backside, but he refused to do this. However he kissed him on his naked flesh at the back of his shoulder, and he told him that all this was in the rules of the order. . . .

To 36–39 he replied that the initiation took place secretly, with doors and windows closed, and no one present except the brothers of the order; and for four years, he said, before he entered the order, he heard it said that they kissed each other on the backside, and that this was reported of many of them in many places; the witness himself did not believe this, he said, because if he had believed it he would never have entered the order. . . .

To 46–47, concerning idols, he replied that a few years before his initiation he had heard it reported by many that when a chapter of the Templars was celebrated in Paris, a head appeared to them in the middle of the night, and was greatly venerated. After his initiation he heard nothing more about it, and did not believe it . . . but he heard it said, after he was in the order, that the said brother Radulphus had a familiar spirit, whose advice was wise and valuable.

The question of the value of the statements in the trial of the Templars has been discussed in detail by historians. Hans Prutz,[109] for example, takes an extreme point of view; according to him the records suggest that the Templars had adopted a dualistic Cathar doctrine, and were thus to be regarded as heretics. Henry Charles Lea, on the other hand, thinks it most unlikely 'that a rich, worldly and ambitious body like the Templars should secretly engage in a dangerous and eccentric attempt to found a new religion which could bring them no advantage, and owing to the vast probability of discovery could bring them certain ruin. If we are really taking this point of view, we must attribute to the Templars an enthusiasm and willingness for martyrdom which we might expect from the asceticism of a Cathar or a Dolcinist, but not from an order the worldly bias of which was the real cause of its downfall.'[110] Lea, however, goes to the other extreme, as he regards all the statements as virtually worthless. He considers the initiation rites as nothing but exaggerated trials of unconditional obedience.[111] As the question of historical accuracy is not of essential importance for a phenomenological study, this controversy is not really our concern. We can say, however, in agreement with certain scholars who prefer to avoid both extremes, that two definite points can be made: first that in some respects the initiation rites of the Templars are in the tradition of male secret societies, and secondly that, under the influence of Near-Eastern Islamic philosophy, with which it was in continual contact, the Order of the Temple had developed features alien to the accepted dogma of the Church. Since these features were considered godless – belonging, in fact, to the Devil – the initiation rites of the Templars can reasonably be seen as a form of Satan worship. The following story is significant: On 19 April 1311, Pierre de la Palu, a Dominican monk and a graduate in theology from the diocese of Lyons, declared that he possessed information on the Templars. This was his statement for the records: At the beginning of the order two knights, sitting on the same horse, had fought together. The one seated in front commended himself to Jesus Christ and was wounded; the other, behind him, said he would commend himself to one who could help him better, and was not wounded.

After the fight the victor, who must have been the Devil in human form, said to the vanquished: 'If you are willing to believe in me, the order will multiply and become rich.' The other let himself be led astray, and so began the errors of the Order of the Temple.[112]

The ritual of the kiss is similar to the corresponding ceremony at the witches' sabbath. De Lancre says the Devil was kissed not only on his buttocks, but often on his face and his navel (also his penis). The backbone seems here to take the place of the buttocks. The navel has a special mana as the centre of the body and the junction of the child to the mother, which is why it has acquired great importance in various techniques of meditation.[113] The kiss on the navel brings the initiate into symbolical contact with the 'maternal' tradition of the order, present in the Master. It is also possible that homosexual eroticism played a part (according to some statements, sexual relationships between members of the order were freely permitted) but it remains in the background. After the ritual of the kiss, the central ceremonies follow.

The rite of the cross probably owes much to Islamic influence. This becomes clear if we refer to certain passages in the trial records stating the reasons given to the novice for the command to spit on the cross and tread it underfoot. The cross, he was told, is only a piece of wood, and *Dominus noster* is *in coelis* – Our Lord is in Heaven.[114] The Islamic prohibition on making images of God has the same reason. Early Christianity also rejected the veneration of images, and later this question led to the great iconoclast movement. If the rite is interpreted in this way, the renunciation of Jesus is really a rejection of the representation of the Son of God in material images. The ritual of the cross is thus a deliberate antithesis to the dogma of the Church, and a reaction against the cult of crucifixes and pictures in the Christian Church of the Middle Ages. This explanation, it is true, touches on only one aspect of this obscure rite, especially as the order puts another image in the place of the cross – the mysterious head.

The head, most often referred to as the 'Head of Baphomet',[115] appears in many forms in the statements: with glowing carbuncles for eyes, with several faces, in animal form, and so on. Its magical power was so great that many Templars said that at the sight of it they became deeply confused and trembled uncontrollably. The cord tied round it received some of this power. A variety of interpretations of the head have been given – the incarnation of

Muhammad, Allah, the Christian God of creation, the Devil, and so on.[116] Even if none of these explanations is entirely convincing, the question of the archetype represented by the head can perhaps be answered. The bearded male head is probably an embodiment of the dark chthonic side of the primeval male element, which, like the corresponding aspect of the female element, was largely rejected in Christian societies. This aspect of the male element is also personified in Satan, but there is a difference between him and the head. The figure of Satan represents a 'later', distorted and dualistcally one-sided version of the male element; the head goes back to a more ancient, deeper level. Moreover, the head is often shown as androgynous: at the ultimate, primeval level, the male and female elements are one.

At this point we can glance back at the ritual of the cross. We can now see another point of view: the Church's conventional image of the God-Man is to be erased from the novice's mind so that he can be dedicated to a more primitive mystery. Possibly, the head, which appears to be made of silver, copper or gold, may also have reference to the power and wealth of the order. The great mass of the Knights of the Temple, particularly in the later years of the order, was flatly materialistic, but somehow there exists in the 'worldliness' of the Templars something of the power of the chthonic male element, in contrast to the entirely spiritual Christ-figure, which is not of this world.

6 THE PRIVATE CHARACTER OF THE BLACK MASS AT THE TIME OF LOUIS XIV

It was obvious even in the writing of de Lancre that the Satan cult was beginning to invade the churches. At the time of Louis XIV this process reached its natural conclusion; the ritual was no longer public, but took place only in restricted circles. The importance of individuals thus became greater than it had been earlier.

A *The confessions of Magdelaine Bavent*

The seventeenth century saw instances of Satanism in religious communities; among the names involved were those of the priests Louis Gaufridy, Urbain Grandier and Jean-Baptiste Girard, and the Ursulines played a special part.[1] We have selected the example containing the greatest number of elements of the cult – the affair of the nuns at Louviers in Normandy. It also belongs partly to the history of the witches' sabbath.

According to the confession that Sister Magdelaine Bavent, who held the office of portress, made to the Bishop of Evreux in 1647,[2] extraordinarily sinister things had been happening in the convent for fourteen years. The former father confessor of the convent, David by name, who had died in the meantime, had held the theory that sin must be driven out by sin, and had led a number of sisters into improper behaviour, including lesbianism. Since he was also of the opinion that the conditions of Paradise should be reproduced, he had made the sisters go naked in the kitchen and the garden, and sent them to communion stripped to the waist. He had also committed sacrilege, for example by having consecrated hosts thrown on to the dunghill. His successor Picard, who had also died, had gone a great deal further than his predecessor. He had made a blood-pact with the Devil, dishonoured the sacred host in a variety of ways, and induced the nuns to take part in the sabbath. The business continued under his successor Boullé. When Magdelaine Bavent made her general confession, fourteen out of fifty-two sisters felt themselves to be possessed by the Devil. Magdelaine, who was considered the ringleader, and on whose body four witch-marks were found, was sentenced to imprisonment for life. Boullé and another priest were burnt at the stake in 1647, and the exhumed body of Picard was burnt with them. The rest of the nuns were divided between different convents.

We give some extracts from the confession, which contains an abundance of detail:

Histoire de Magdelaine Bavent, Religieuse du Monastère de Saint-Louis de Louviers, etc., Paris 1672, Chap. IX, p. 29.

I say, then, that the evil-doing, mainly of the priests who attend these night-time assemblies, reaches such a point that they often bring hosts consecrated in the church, and place them on a kind of altar which is there, then they say their Mass; afterwards they take them up again, take out a circle from the centre, the size of a quarter-crown, put them on to a piece of vellum or parchment, pierced and cut out in the same way, and stick them down with a sort of grease resembling pitch. Then they pass them over their private parts as far up as the belly, and in this state abandon themselves to the company of women. . . .

ibid., p. 31

On Maundy Thursday I saw the Lord's Supper being celebrated in a horrible way. A roasted child was brought in. It was eaten by the assembly, and I could not say with certainty whether I tasted it. I told my Confessor that I thought I had, and that I stopped eating at once because this meat was tasteless. But the most remarkable thing was that during this disgusting feast a demon went round the table crying *Not one of you will betray me.* I myself believe that with these words they are renewing their intention not to accuse each other, so as to be faithful to the Devil.

ibid., p. 52

On the Sabbath they cast many evil spells, compounded of sacred hosts, the blood that sometimes drips from them, and the principal internal parts of the bodies of children, or of other dead people. I do not know if any other drug goes in. They are like little balls, and I cannot think of any other name for them. Picard often made them. . . .

The custom described in the first passage is very impressive. It is a kind of Satanic 'sacred marriage rite' in which the priest seeks to give divine power to his masculinity. If the only purpose were to dishonour the host, the ceremonious preparation would not be necessary. The rest fits into what has already been said.

B *The masses of the Abbé Guibourg and his associates*

On the instigation of the Commissioner of Police Nicholas de la Reynie, Louis XIV set up, on 8 March 1679, a commission to investigate extremely strange and sinister proceedings in which even people in the King's immediate entourage were involved. This so-called *Commission de l'Arsenal* held its sessions, which were secret, in a room hung with black cloth and lit with candles, and so went down to history under the name of *Chambre ardente.*[3]

This case rests on a solid basis of historical facts, which we shall leave until we come to the interpretation. We shall begin by quoting a series of extracts from the records of the commission (only the last passage refers to a later period).

Bastille Archives, Interrogation of Lesage, Vincennes, 28 November 1679. (Ravaisson VI, pp. 55ff)

He met the priest Davot for the first time at the house of La Voisin. . . .

When Madame de Vivien was at the house of La Voisin, and asked him to pass a note in which she demanded the death of her husband and the friendship of a certain abbé, Davot promised the lady that when he said Mass he would put the note under the corporal and under the chalice; but he [Lesage] kept the note in his hands and did not give it to Davot. The lady gave Davot a gold crown or gold louis. . . . Davot and La Voisin both told him that he had said Mass in La Voisin's private room on the belly of a girl or woman whom he would be able to remember in the course of time, and Davot also said that he had had carnal knowledge of her, and that while saying Mass he had kissed her private parts, and that he was not the only one to do such things, and that Gérard, priest of Saint-Sauveur, Davot's friend, with whom he [Lesage] had eaten and drunk at Davot's house, had also said Mass on the belly of a shopkeeper's daughter from the Rue

Saint-Denis, in the parish of Saint-Sauveur, whom he had debauched and whom he had persuaded that when he performed the ceremony and some conjurations on her belly, she would not become pregnant, but the girl, after remaining hidden for some time at Gérard's in a garret, did become pregnant, and Gérard was worried about it, and disappeared after remaining hidden for a time in Davot's house at Saint-Benoit. . . .

(Bibliothèque de l'Arsenal)

Interrogation of La Voisin's daughter, Vincennes, 28 March 1680. Marie-Marguerite Montvoisin, aged twenty-one.
ibid., p. 194

Lesage and her mother sent her one day, she could not say whether it was in Lent, to buy a live white pigeon, which she did with a 15-sou piece; after she had done this, and brought it to them, they cut its throat and collected its blood in a glass goblet. They kept this blood, and sent her out of the garden-house where this was going on, so that she does not know what they did with it. . . .

She does not know whether the blood and heart of the pigeon were mixed with holy water; but it is true that he [Lesage] in these ceremonies used incense, salt, sulphur and holy water which he mixed together; and it is also true that a cross which was at her [her mother's] house, and in which there is some of the True Cross of Jerusalem, was used in the ceremonies carried out by Lesage and her mother; and she does not know if it was used that time – this was after Lesage came back from the galleys – and this was done for the marriage of the Desmarets woman, for Madame Brisard's affairs, and for other affairs which they had. . . .

(Bibliothèque de l'Arsenal)

Interrogation of La Filastre, Vincennes, 26 May 1680
ibid., pp. 211ff

. . . – Was it not true that suffering the pains of childbirth, she placed herself in a circle around which there were candles lit, holding in her hand a black candle, also lit?

– Simon made her sit down on the edge of the circle, telling her that the spirits were within, and that one of the candles was for

Пiите отъ нея вси

ЧУДО В КАНЕ ГАЛИЛЕЙСКОЙ
ИЛИ ОТКУДА ПОШЛА САМОГОНКА

(Евангелие от Иоанна. Гл. II, стихи 1—10).

Во дни оны, отложив попечение житейское.
Пошел Иисус на свадьбу в Кану Галилейскую (Иоан II,1).
Иде же, в место веселия,
У всех было огорчение велие.
Поелику у гостей—выпить была охота велика,
Вино же они сожрали все до последнего глотка!
И рече господь: Слушайте люди,
Какие же вы, однако, ротозеи!
Ну, и народ, доложу я вам, в этой сторонке!
Ни кто не имеет понятия о самогонке!
Вина нет? Да это еще пол-беды,
Давайте скорей сюда бочку воды.
Я даю вам честное слово,
В одну минуту вино будет готово.
Тащите ко мне порожнюю посуду,
Сейчас сотворю я великое чудо.
Сие бо есть не обман и не сказка-
У меня как раз с собою закваска.

И возопили к нему: услыши нас, господи и скажи,
Какой самый лучший рецепт ханжи.
И излил господь закваску в окоренок—по милости своей велицей
И стал разводить, ее доливая водицей
„Се сотвори начаток знамением Иисус...—и яви свою славу" (И. II, 2)
И напоил ханжой всю ораву.
„И уверовали в него ученики его" (И. II 2), яко
Сотвори господь, без обмана,
Ибо „как стелька" в тот день все были пьяны.
И сам „архитриклин"*) яко же вкуси
Вина, бывшего от воды" (И. II, 9),
Стал к стене и не двигался „ни туды ни сюды".
И рече архитриклин: благословен господь от Сиона.
Давай нам рецепт самогона!

*) Распорядитель.

Anti-religious version of the Marriage in Cana (page from the *Besboshnik*), from Fülöp-Miller, *Geist und Gesicht des Bolshewismus* (Amalthea-Verlag, Vienna, 1926)

'Mon caveau', oil painting by Clovis Trouille, *c.* 1930 (in the possession of the artist)

Lucifer, and another for another devil, whose name she does not remember, and so on with the other candles, and she did not hold the candle of black pitch in her hand, although it was lit. Simon made her say among other things, that Briziol [God of dream interpretation and soothsaying] was to come in the name of Picart and Simon, and made her renounce the chrism, baptism, and the Church; after that she said some more words which she does not remember. And the conjuration was written by the hand of Picart. . . .

– Did Simon not make her say some other words as well, and, among others: in the name of the great living God and of the Holy Trinity, by St Peter and by St Paul, and that the Devil must appear?

– Yes, but she does not remember that these words St Peter and St Paul were written down in the conjuration; and there were many other more disgusting words, and, among others, renunciations of the Holy Sacrament, the Mass, the sacred host, holy water, and her baptism; Simon made her learn these words by heart, and then burnt the paper; and after teaching them to her, Simon made her say them three and a half months after her confinement, in a church to which she took her, near the Louvre on the side nearest the river; and this went on for nine days, and when she said them, she made her turn towards the holy water basin, and enter and leave the church several times. . . .

– Is it not true that she attended some Masses which were said at night in Maître Jean's house?

– It is true that Cotton, priest of St Paul's and schoolmaster, came about five or six years ago, on a Maundy Thursday, to the house of Maître Jean, who was then porter at the Quinze-Vingts [hospital in Paris]; and in the night between Maundy Thursday and Good Friday, at midnight, Cotton, dressed in priest's robes, said Mass in a little room over the porter's room. Present at the Mass were herself and Lalande, who said the responses, while Lecourt, who had brought Cotton, was outside with Maître Jean, who had brought the vestments and the altar furniture to his room for use at the Mass, at which Cotton consecrated a host, performed the elevation and invoked the three princes of the demons in unintelligible words; and Cotton had the invocation, which consisted of few words, in writing on the altar, which had been set up for the purpose, and after the invocation he finished the Mass in this place, and wrapped the consecrated host in a corporal-cloth he had brought. And she had never since asked him what he had done with the host. . . .

She has heard tell that the Dufayet woman had had some strange things done by Lepreux, and that while celebrating Mass he had consecrated snakes for use in secret love-potions, and that Duplessis was present at the time. . . .

Declaration by Voisin's daughter, 20 August 1680.
ibid., p. 294ff.

. . . She saw Guibourg celebrate two Masses in the room where her mother slept, and one at Delaporte's house, where she, Montvoisin, arrived at the moment when he was finishing; she saw the altar set up, with a cross and lighted candles. The three Masses were said for the same affair, this last one between two and three in the afternoon, two months before her mother was arrested. Guibourg said Masses on ladies' bellies at her mother's house. The first to her knowledge was more than six years ago; she helped her mother to prepare the things necessary for it – a mattress on chairs, two stools, one at each side, where the candlesticks with candles stood; when this was done, Guibourg came out of the little side room dressed in his chasuble, and after that La Voisin brought into the room the woman on whose belly Mass was to be celebrated, and sent her, Montvoisin, out.

When she was older her mother was no longer cautious with her, and she was present at this sort of Mass, and saw that the lady was placed completely naked on the mattress, with her head hanging back supported on a pillow on an overturned chair, her legs hanging down, a towel on her belly, and on the towel a cross at the level of her lower ribs, and the chalice on her belly.

Madame de Montespan had a Mass of this sort said for her by Guibourg at La Voisin's house about three years ago. She came at about ten at night and did not leave until midnight.

And when La Voisin told the lady that she must fix a time for the other two Masses that had to be said if her affair was to succeed, the lady said that she could not find the time, and that she would have to do without her whatever had to be done for the success of her affair; she [La Voisin] promised this, and that she would have the two Masses celebrated on herself, on behalf of her, Madame de Montespan.

Some time later she attended a Mass which Guibourg celebrated in the same way on her mother's belly, and at the elevation he spoke the name of Louis de Bourbon and that of the lady, which consisted of two or three names, and he did not say that of Montespan.

The woman Laporte attended the first [Mass] with her and her mother, and spoke the responses; she slept at her house and knew very well who the lady was, although she bore witness that she did not know her.

Laporte, for the same purpose, made a conjuration to the soul of a hanged man; her mother had given her the names in writing in order to do it, and when she had done it she came to give an account in the presence of her father and brothers. The father silenced Laporte.

And the second [Mass], celebrated by proxy, Laporte and the Pelletier woman attended with her.

The third was celebrated at Delaporte's house and in her presence; she [Voisin's daughter] did not arrive until it was all over. The candles were of new yellow wax, fat from a hanged man, and a note was put into them, the invention of Papillon, and at both Masses at her [Delaporte's] house, Guibourg put powders under the chalice, and said they were for love, and afterwards gave them to her mother.

La Voisin had other priests working for the same business, as well as Guibourg. . . .

(Bibliothèque Nationale)

Interrogation of Voisin's daughter, Vincennes, 9 October 1680
ibid., p. 333f

. . . She remembered that Pelletier brought two afterbirths to Saint-Denis, on two different occasions, to Guibourg, priest, one of which was later distilled by Pelletier and the other by Dumesnil. It is also true that a midwife who lived at the corner of the Rue des Deux-Portes, also distilled the entrails of a child which the mother had borne there, brought by Voisin, her mother, for an abortion. Before the distillation, the child's entrails and the mother's afterbirth had been taken to Saint-Denis, to Guibourg, by her mother, the midwife, and the child's mother, on whose belly her mother on her return said Guibourg had celebrated Mass, and that the woman was then still all covered with blood. . . .

Guibourg baptised at her mother's a child of a girl whom Lepère aborted. She saw three or four children burnt up in the oven. A child that appeared to have been prematurely born was presented at Madame de Montespan's Mass by order of her mother, and Guibourg put it into a basin, cut its throat, poured the blood into a chalice and consecrated it with the host, finished his Mass, then took out the child's entrails; the next day mother Voisin took to Dumesnil, to be distilled, the blood and the host in a glass phial which Madame de Montespan took away. The child's body was burnt in the stove by mother Voisin. . . .

. . . She believes that Dumesnil had brought the child for Madame de Montespan's Mass.

At the consecration, Guibourg said the names of the King and those of Madame de Montespan.

(Bibliothèque Nationale)

Extract from the interrogation of the Abbé Guibourg, Vincennes, 10 October 1680.
ibid., p. 335f

Leroy, governor of the pages of the *petite écurie*, first spoke to him about working for Madame de (Montespan) and promised him 50 pistoles and a benefice of 2,000 pounds. The first Mass he said with this intention was at Le Ménil near Montlhéry, on the belly of a woman who had come with another great personage; at the consecration he recited the conjuration:

(Bibliothèque du Corps Législatif)

'Astaroth, Asmodeus, princes of friendship, I conjure you to accept the sacrifice I offer you of this child for the things I ask of you, which are that the friendship of the King and Mgr le Dauphin may continue towards me, and that I may be honoured by the princes and princesses of the court, and that nothing I ask of the King may be denied me, either for my relatives or servants.'

(Bibliothèque Nationale)

And he named the names of the King and those of Madame de Montespan, which were in the conjuration.

He had bought for a crown the child that was sacrificed at this Mass; it was presented to him by a grown girl. Having drawn blood from the child, whose throat he pierced with a penknife, he poured some into the chalice, after which the child was removed and taken to another place, and its heart and entrails were brought back to him for a second [Mass]; according to what Leroy and the noble lord said, they would serve to make powders for the (King) and Madame de (Montespan). The lady for whom he said Mass always had the veils of her headdress pulled low, covering her face and half her breast. He said the second Mass in a hovel on the ramparts of Saint-Denis, on the same woman with the same ceremonies and Pelletier was there. He celebrated the third in Paris, at La Voisin's house, on the same woman, perhaps eight or nine years ago; later he said thirteen or fourteen years. He also declares that five years ago he said a similar Mass at La Voisin's on the same person, who, he was always told, was (Madame de Montespan), for the same intention, and Laporte was present; and after it was all over he went to pick up his cloak from a chair and found on the chair a document which must have been a copy of a pact – since it was only on paper, and pacts must be written on virgin parchment – where he read these words:

(Bibliothèque du Corps Législatif)

'I . . . daughter of . . . I ask for the King's friendship and that of Mgr le Dauphin, and that I may continue to have it, that the Queen may be barren, that the King may leave her bed and table for me, that I may obtain from him all I ask for myself and my relatives, that my servants and my household may please him, [that I may be] loved and respected by great lords, that I may be summoned to the King's council and know what happens there, and that this friendship may increase more than in the past, so that the King leaves La Vallière and pays no more attention to her, and that the Queen may be repudiated so that I can marry the King. . . .

(Bibliothèque Nationale)

And when he got to this point in his reading this paper was snatched from his hands; he always left the host and the consecrated blood of the children in vessels that were given him, the host being cut into small pieces.

At La Voisin's, dressed in alb, stole and maniple, he made a conjuration in the presence of Des Œillets, who wanted to make a charm for the (King) and who was accompanied by a man who gave him the conjuration, and, as it was necessary to have sperm from both sexes, Des Œillets who was menstruating could not give any, but she poured some of her menstrual blood into the chalice, and the man accompanying her passing into the alcove behind the bed with him, Guibourg, dropped some of his sperm into the chalice. On top of all this, Des Œillets and the man each put a powder of bat's blood and flour to give a firmer consistency to the whole compound, and after reciting the conjuration he took it all out of the chalice and it was put into a little vessel which Des Œillets or the man took away.

(Bibliothèque du Corps Législatif)

Notes for a report from M. de la Reynie to the King (November 1680). ibid., pp. 371f

. . . La Voisin's daughter, questioned again on the further Mass which, as she said, Madame de Montespan had had celebrated by this same Guibourg at her mother's only three or four years ago, declared all the circumstances:

That it was she who had presented the child to Guibourg, that the woman Delaporte was present, and that after the oblation, when the blood had been put into the chalice, Guibourg had gone into another room and opened the breast and torn out the heart and entrails.

Guibourg, who had denied opening the child's body, agreed that he had torn out the heart and entrails and had cut open the child's heart after the Mass to take out the clotted blood that was inside the heart and put it into a vessel prepared for that purpose; and with it he also put fragments of the consecrated host, and what was in the chalice, and it was taken away by the lady on whose belly he had celebrated Mass, whom he believed to be Madame de Montespan, as La Voisin told him. . .

(Bibliothèque Nationale)

Autograph notes by M. d'Argenson (1695).
ibid., VII, pp. 172f

Marianne Charmillon, aged 22, daughter of Charmillon, practician [assistant to an advocate] in Paris, and of Mme Quenneville, at present a voluntary penitent at Sainte-Pélagie, said, in the presence of the Mother Superior and a commissioner at the Châtelet, that she had been seduced and corrupted by J. B. Sebault, subdeacon of the diocese of Bourges, who lodged at her father's house, and by whom she has had two children, still alive; that two years ago this same Sebault proposed that she should make a pact with the Devil, and took her for that purpose into the cellar of a house on the outskirts of Paris, where the invocation, the apparition and the conclusion were to take place; that she had been in this same cellar on six different occasions and that Mass was said there between midnight and one o'clock; that the first time a beggar girl aged 13 was brought there and died of fright, and was buried with her clothes by the said Guignard, vicar of Notre-Dame de Bourges, and another private individual; that Guignard said Mass in priest's vestments; that he celebrated it once on the body of the penitent, naked, without a shift, and that the subdeacon Sebault, who was naked as she was, said the responses to the Mass. As often as the altar had to be kissed, Guignard kissed Charmillon's body, and consecrated the host on her private parts, into which he inserted a fragment of the host; when the Mass was at last ended, the subdeacon Sebault entered into her, and meanwhile Guignard and his friend also copulated with a woman called Lefebvre. When the Mass was over, Sebault plunged his hands into the chalice and washed his private parts and the woman's. Guignard, this other individual and Lefebvre did the same. After this Guignard put what remained in the chalice into a little phial which he carried away carefully. . . .

(Bibliothèque Nationale)

The sinister happenings reported in these trial records are in impressive contrast to the glittering magnificence of the French court, at the centre of which stood the *Roi Soleil* – the Sun King. Louis XIV received this name, which has become the symbol of the whole epoch, after playing the part of the Sun in 1653 in the

Ballet Royal de la Nuit.[4] The libretto of this masque gave the King the following words to speak:

> I am the source of light,
> And the most renowned stars
> Whose circle surrounds me
> Are brilliant and respected
> Only by the splendour that I give them.[5]

This, in secular form, is the Christian sun-symbolism, in which Christ, who referred to himself as the 'Light of the world' (John 8: 12) is the *sol verus* – the true sun – and *fons luminis* – the source of light.[6] The King becomes a secular counterpart of Christ, and his court corresponds to the court of Heaven. The facts that form the subject of this chapter bear out the proverb which says that the brightest light brings the darkest shadows. The Satan worship and black magic which were to be found in the King's immediate circle existed in compensation for the principles embodied in Louis XIV.

In the Paris of that period it was the general practice, especially in exalted circles, to use poison or the black arts to get rid of rivals, unwanted spouses, relatives whose property one wished to inherit, and so on. The black mass too was pressed into the service of magic; it was used to dispose of people who were in the way and to win the favour of those to whose love one aspired. Here we meet two new facts in the history of the Satan cult. It is interesting from a sociological point of view that the emphasis shifts to members of the aristocracy, who make use of the black mass in their struggle for social and erotic prestige; and the Satanic rites were carried out with a definite purpose in view. We must emphasise that the affairs dealt with in the *Chambre ardente* represent only one aspect – though the most important – of the Satanic practices of this period.

For easier understanding we are dividing the commentary according to the separate sections.

Interrogation of Lesage, 28 November 1679

La Voisin (original name Cathérine Deshayes, Montvoisin by marriage) was one of the famous sorceresses in Paris. All the world came to her little house in the Rue La Villeneuve-sur-Gravois to have their fortunes told and their hands read, to obtain poison or procure abortions. In addition she had priests at her disposal for the celebration of the black mass, such as Davot, who appears here. The witness Lesage, a wool merchant, was her most active assistant. He was sentenced to the galleys in 1668, but released five years later, through Voisin's influence. In this phase of the Satan cult, too, belief in the effectiveness of ecclesiastical rites, particularly the consecration, remains unshaken. So also does the conviction that a renegade priest, or one living in mortal sin, retains his priestly powers.

What is the significance of the woman's naked body used as an altar?

The symbolism of the altar is predominantly female. Originally it was none other than the hearth, which is matriarchal in character.[7] The symbolism is as follows: the woman as the vessel that receives, transforms and brings forth (the womb in the broadest sense) – the hearth as the place where food is transformed and prepared – the altar as the place of consecration and preparation of 'celestial food'. The Christian sees the female aspect of the altar in a different way. The altar[8] is for him the prototype of the communion table, and an image of Christ's cross. But both the food-bearing table and the cross (see above p. 81) have maternal characteristics. And we can go further.

> The deepest symbolic meaning of the altar lies in its anointing. It is expressed in Psalm 45, which . . . accompanies this holy ceremony [the dedication of the altar]. This psalm is a royal wedding-song, celebrating the King's marriage with his bride, Christ's marriage with the Church. The altar is the consecrated bridal couch, specially prepared by God in this holy anointing. Upon it takes place, at every holy sacrifice, the mysterious marriage of Christ with his Church.[9]

Thus in the altar the female motif is fused with that of *coniunctio* or union. So, when a woman's body serves as altar for the black mass, it is an instinctive and quite literal realisation of this symbolism; and the same applies to the sexual rites accompanying it. The urge to increase to its utmost the magical effectiveness of the black mass leads to an unconscious regression to a significance given to the altar in very ancient times, and to a corresponding practice, consciously anti-Church. A purely sexual explanation is by no means enough, for the participants in Satanic rites would certainly not have needed ceremonies like this to help them to enjoy sexual fulfilment.

Interrogation of Voisin's daughter, 28 March 1680

In ancient times the dove was sacred to Ishtar-Aphrodite-Venus, and so was used in love spells from a very early stage.[10] Blood sorcery will be discussed later.

Interrogation of La Filastre, 26 May 1680

Françoise Filastre was a god-daughter of La Voisin, and, after her, the most respected black magician in Paris. The women Simon and Dufayet belonged to Voisin's and Filastre's circle. The report on the black mass shows that the priests only strove to gain mana by consecration in order to use it in acts of magic. (The consecration of adders, which is also mentioned, is not valid from a Church point of view, but is connected with snake symbolism.) Something is, as it were, 'abstracted' from Christ, so that the superhuman power, as it becomes present, can be used directly in the service of Satan. It is thus possible to couple the elevation with the invocation of demons. As far as the rite first described is concerned, it is connected with the belief that the process of birth has the special effect of bringing a woman into communication with divine and demonic powers; this is expressed in the folklore and folk customs of every race[11] (for instance the taboo on women after childbirth). La Filastre is, in her condition, especially apt for the evocation of demons. The circle in which she has to sit belongs to an old tradition. Circles of this kind are negative symbols of wholeness; they are formed like a mandala[12] and their function is to concentrate the powers of darkness. La Filastre's child was killed immediately after birth and sacrificed to Satan. There is also in the text a satanic form of the *toties-quoties* indulgence, which is gained whenever anyone comes back to the Church and offers up a prescribed prayer.

Magic Circle for the Evocation of Demons.

Declaration of Voisin's daughter, 20 August 1680

The Marquise Françoise Athénais de Montespan was born in 1641, the daughter of the Duke of Rochechouart. She married a nobleman from her own homeland and became a lady-in-waiting to the Queen. Dazzled by the splendour of the court and fascinated by Louis XIV, she soon set out to oust the King's mistress at the time, Louise de Lavallière. In order to get help to do this, she contacted La Voisin in 1667. In the following year she fulfilled her wish; she became the King's acknowledged mistress, and subsequently bore him seven children, who all had to be legitimised by the Parliament. She maintained her relationship with La Voisin, and each time she suspected that the King intended to deprive her of his grace and favour she availed herself of the sorceress's services. La Voisin procured for Madame de Montespan the Abbé Guibourg, then seventy years old, to hold black masses for her purposes. Guibourg, who is described as cross-eyed and with a red puffy face, was the sacristan of Saint Marcel in Saint-Denis. The first three black masses of which La Voisin's daughter speaks were held in 1673. At this time Louis XIV was suffering severe attacks of giddiness, perhaps as a result of the 'love-powder' which Madame de Montespan obtained from La Voisin and added to his food. The next masses mentioned (three were always considered necessary) took place in 1677 or the beginning of 1678; the third series can be dated 1678 or 1679. There had already, for various reasons, been several crises in the relationship between the King and Madame de Montespan, but during this latter period something happened to throw the Marquise into a real panic. Louis XIV fell in love with Marie-Angélique de Fontanges, and was determined to make her Madame de Montespan's successor. The fact that Madame de Montespan herself served as altar for the masses which Guibourg said for her (Plate 2) must have substantially heightened the effectiveness of the magic in the eyes of the participants.

Interrogation of Voisin's daughter, 9 October 1680

The whole truth came to light only gradually. In the interests of sorcery and the black masses, a large number of babies had been horribly killed. Once when La Voisin was drunk she said she had aborted and burnt 2,500 children,[13] but that is certainly a gross exaggeration. It cannot be estimated how many new-born babies were murdered. We know only details such as the fact that Guibourg killed even his own children by his mistress Chanfrain. When Voisin's daughter was expecting a child she fled into the provinces and did not come back until she had ensured that the new-born baby was safely hidden. The blood ritual has its origin in beliefs and superstitions connected with blood.[14]

Blood has always been considered to be the seat of the soul. Wilhelm Wundt says:

> The irresistible force of this notion is easily understood; . . . a man wounded in battle sees his life ebbing away with the blood that streams from his wound. This conception is reflected in a multiplicity of ways in the customs and usages of many primi-

tive races, as well as in the past history of peoples now civilised. The custom, widespread in primitive cultures, of drinking the blood of a slain enemy or even of a sacrificed animal is the most direct example of this conception of the soul. The strength and courage of the slain warrior are supposed to enter into the man who drinks his blood; and the blood of the sacrifice is thought to confer the superhuman strength of the animal.[15]

The theme of blood has appeared in many forms, from coarse and literal notions to such subtle interpretations as those found, for example, in the Hellenistic period or in the works of Alexandrine theologians. Blood occupies a central place in both the Old and the New Testament. In Lev. 17: 11, we read: 'For the life of the flesh is in the blood, and I have given it to you upon the altar to make an atonement for your souls, for it is the blood that maketh an atonement for the soul.' Blood is also the symbol of the pact that Jehovah makes with his people. Blood as a means of redemption plays a part in various Hellenistic mysteries. The Hellenistic tradition, together with that of the Old Testament, gave rise to the New Testament conception of the redeeming power of Christ's blood, expressed in the mystery of the mass; in the course of time this led to the development of a special mystique in the baroque era, Abbé Guibourg and his friends were regressing to the primitive cannibalistic stage of the belief in the efficacy of blood. The use of the entrails goes back to an old symbolic connection between them and the underworld (in Babylon, where divination by the entrails was customary, the underworld was called *êkal tirâni* – Palace of the Entrails[16]) and thus, in Christian terms, Hell. The distillation of the entrails was supposed to produce a magically effective Satanic 'spirit'.

Extract from the interrogation of Abbé Guibourg, 10 October 1680

Most of this is comprehensible in the light of what has already been said. Des Œillets was a chambermaid of Madame de Montespan. Here we meet the old description of the vaginal fluid as sperm. Sperm and menstrual blood, the substitute for female 'sperm', were traditionally seen as possessing mana. The bat in folklore is a typical beast of the Devil. According to the report – as Ravaisson says[17] – Des Œillets appears to have worked also for

Louis XIV or for Charles II of England (the man accompanying her was an Englishman). But perhaps the word *pour* only means that the stuff was used on Louis XIV on behalf of Madame de Montespan.

Notes for a report by M. de la Reynie to the King (November 1680)

The interrogations were carried out by the Chief of Police in minute detail, with considerable acumen, and without respect of persons. The descriptions of the black mass are therefore absolutely credible.

It was all in vain; the King abandoned Madame de Montespan and made Marie-Angélique de Fontanges his new favourite. Madame de Montespan now determined to kill the King and her rival with La Voisin's help. A petition containing a lethal powder was to be handed to the King, while Mademoiselle de Fontanges was to be given slow-acting poisons in order to create the impression that she was dying of a broken heart over the King's death. The delivery of the petition went wrong, and shortly before the second attempt La Voisin took fright and gave the paper to her daughter to burn. The plot was uncovered a few days later, and La Voisin and the other conspirators were arrested. La Voisin was burnt at the stake in the same year, and six years later the Abbé Guibourg died in prison in the citadel of Besançon.

When Louis XIV learned that Madame de Montespan and other people at court were directly involved in the affair, he dissolved the *Commission de l'Arsenal* in August 1680, so that from then on La Reynie carried on his investigations alone. Later, in 1709, the King had most of the records burnt; however, sufficient copies and a number of important original documents are still extant.

In order to avoid a scandal, the King contented himself with moving Madame de Montespan to another apartment in the palace and treating her with suspicion from then on. In 1681 Mademoiselle de Fontanges died at the age of twenty-two of a lung infection of tubercular origin. She died believing she had been poisoned.

In 1691 Madame de Montespan retired to a convent she had founded, to expiate her sins. She did not find peace until just before her death. She died on 27 May 1707.

In the *Chambre ardente* trials there were, in all, 319 arrests and 104 sentences. Thirty-six people were condemned to death, 34 exiled, 4 sent to the galleys, and 30 of the accused were acquitted.

Autograph notes by M. d'Argenson (1695)

This record shows that later in Louise XIV's reign black masses were still being celebrated. The Latin passage in the form of a rubric is remarkable.

The last person in France to be burnt at the stake for sorcery (in 1745) was the priest Louis Debarez, who had held black masses in order to find hidden treasure.[18]

7 THE ROMANTIC STYLE OF THE SATAN CULT IN THE NINETEENTH CENTURY

When the Satan cult became a private matter at the time of Louis XIV, the way was opened to its next stage of development. In the nineteenth century it became individual and literary. By this we do not mean that the Satan cult or elements of it became the subject of literary works (as happened – to take examples from different periods – with Tasso, de Sade, Joyce and Genet); we refer to the composition in verse of prayers to Satan or blasphemies, that is to say the poetic elevation of verbal elements of the Satan cult.

The evolution of the Satan cult, which we are demonstrating with the help of three texts, must be seen against the background of the romantic literature in which the Devil became a central figure. Although we cannot go into this here, it is discussed in detail in the work by Mario Praz, *La carne, la morte e il diavolo nella letteratura romantica*.[1]

A *Baudelaire's* 'Litanies de Satan'

In Paris in 1846, a group of young people was formed who, in revolt against the social and religious standards of their time, met every Sunday for Satan worship.[2] Charles Baudelaire was closely associated with this circle, and his 'Litanies de Satan', included in *Les Fleurs du Mal*, were written in this atmosphere.

Charles Baudelaire, Les Litanies de Satan, from Les Fleurs du Mal, Paris 1857, (Adam, pp. 146ff)

O thou, the wisest and
fairest of the Angels,
God betrayed by Fate and
robbed of praise,

O Satan, have pity on my
long misery!

O Prince of exile, victim
of great wrong,

Who, vanquished, risest
again in greater strength,

O Satan, have pity on my
long misery!

Thou who knowest all, great
King of the underworld,
Familiar healer of human
anguish,

O Satan, have pity on my
long misery!

Thou who, even to lepers, to
outcasts accursed
Teachest through love the
desire for Paradise,

O Satan, have pity on my
long misery!

O thou who, with Death, thine
old invincible mistress,
Didst beget Hope, that
lovely fool,

O Satan, have pity on my
long misery!

Thou who givest to the outlaw
that calm and haughty gaze
That condemns the whole throng
around a scaffold,

O Satan, have pity on my
long misery!

Thou who knowest in what corners
of the envious earth
The jealous God hid the
precious stones,

O Satan, have pity on my
long misery!

Thou whose clear eye knows the
deep arsenals
Where, buried, sleeps the
race of metals,

O Satan, have pity on my
long misery!

Thou whose broad hand hides
the abysses
From the sleepwalker wandering
on the margin of the buildings,

O Satan, have pity on my
long misery!

Thou who by magic makest supple
the old bones
Of the late-lingering drunkard
trampled by the horses,

O Satan, have pity on my
long misery!

Thou who, to comfort feeble
suffering man,
Taughtest us to mix saltpetre
and sulphur

O Satan, have pity on my
long misery!

Thou who signest with thy
mark, O subtle accomplice,
The forehead of Croesus,
pitiless and vile,

O Satan, have pity on my
long misery!

Thou who puttest into
harlots' eyes and hearts
The cult of the wound and the
love of rags,

O Satan, have pity on my
long misery!

Staff of exiles, lamp of
discoverers,
Confessor of hanged men and
conspirators,

O Satan, have pity on my
long misery!

Adoptive father of those whom
in his black rage
God the Father thrust forth
from the Earthly Paradise,

O Satan, have pity on my
long misery!

Prayer

Glory and praise to thee
Satan, in the heights
Of Heaven, where thou hast
reigned, and in the depths
Of Hell where, vanquished,
thou dreamest in silence!
Let my soul one day, beneath
the Tree of Knowledge,
Rest beside thee, at the hour
when over thy brow
Like a new Temple its
branches shall spread!

For Baudelaire, the evil personified in Satan is a reality. He writes at one point: 'I have always been obsessed by the impossibility of understanding certain subordinate actions or thoughts of man without postulating the intervention of an evil force outside himself.'[3] The poet is steeped in Christian dualistic doctrine. At another point he says: 'In every man at every moment there are two simultaneous drives, one towards God, the other towards Satan. The call to God or spirituality is a desire to rise upwards;

that to Satan or sensuality is the pleasure of falling downwards.'[4] Jean-Paul Sartre in his essay on Baudelaire[5] speaks of that *choix originel* by which the poet has opted for loneliness and 'otherness'. With the freedom he has thus won he chooses 'sensuality' and *descent*, and identifies himself with evil. But, says Sartre, in this identification good is recognised; evil, without ceasing to be itself, dignifies by its very existence the thing it opposes, and revolt is a negative glorification of order. So Baudelaire's is only a limited aloneness; it is 'like the feeble image'[6] of the great loneliness of truly free men. In other words, Baudelaire, like all Satanists, is deeply attached to the Christian tradition. He has, however, taken the split to its extreme by following unconditionally one of the 'drives' he recognises, and accepting the destiny it involves. Sartre describes this destiny as 'the deep-rooted dissatisfaction of the fallen God'.[7] This means that Baudelaire is racked by something of the immense tension that marks the dualistic Christian culture, and it is from this tension that his poetry grows.

The 'Litanies de Satan' have the liturgical form of a psalm, with an antiphon recurring after each couplet. The end is a kind of doxology, the beginning of which corresponds to the 'Gloria in excelsis Deo' and the ending of which is a prayer. For Baudelaire, Satan is morally superior to God, because, although betrayed and unjustly treated, he did not lose his dignity and pride. Unlike the noise of the witches' sabbath, the Satanic sphere is here characterised by 'silence'. Satan appears as king of the underworld, a Christian *Zeus Katachtonios* – Zeus below the earth. In his kingdom lie hidden the magical secrets from which Christian consciousness is estranged. He is the comforter and helper of all those oppressed and rejected by Christian society, the pariahs such as Baudelaire feels himself to be. In this we see clear social-revolutionary features. Adam[8] rightly points out that the passage about the mixing of saltpetre and sulphur is without doubt a reference to the February revolution of 1848 and the following period, for the poor were able, with the help of gunpowder, to rise against the rich. The symbol for the latter is Croesus (the original word in the manuscript was 'banquier'). Since God has sided with the rich, just, sober and pure, the 'weary and burdened', the poor, the criminal, drunkards and prostitutes can find 'refreshment' only from the Lord of the Deep. And since God is on the side of reason, Satan has become the source of all irrational, earthly powers.

The 'Litanies de Satan' are in no wise aggressive or blasphemous. There is a peculiar sadness in them – the sadness of one who knows without a doubt that the perfect wholeness, for whose sake he has scorned the heights and chosen the miseries of the depths, will remain for ever beyond his grasp. Only the final 'at the hour' points to a hope that is no longer 'foolish'. The last lines contain the idea of the *Apokatastasis hapantōn*, the 'reintegration of everything' (even the Devil), a theme which has occupied Christian thinkers since the time of Origen.

B *Satanic hymns by G. Leopardi and G. Carducci*

1 Giacomo Leopardi,[9] who died in Naples in 1837 at the age of thirty-nine, wrote, not long before his death, a Satanic hymn which was never finished and was not published until 1868.

Giacomo Leopardi, Ad Arimane, probably written in 1833 (Leopardi, Opere I, pp. 434f)

King of things, creator of the world, secret
Malice, highest power and highest
Intelligence, eternal
Giver of evil and ruler of movement.

I do not know if this makes you happy, but look and enjoy, etc., watching eternally, etc.

production and destruction, etc. To kill, it brings forth, etc. System of the world, all suffering. Nature is like a child that at once destroys what it has made. Old age. Boredom or passions full of pain and desperation: love.

Savages and primitive tribes recognise only you, in different forms. But civilised races, etc. The people call you by different names, Fate, nature and God. But you are Ahriman, you who, etc.

And the civilised world calls to you.

I say nothing of the tempests, the pestilences, etc., your gifts, since you can give nothing else. You give heat and ice.

And the world seeks wildly for new orders and laws, and hopes for perfection. But your work remains unchanging, because by the nature of man, impudence and deception will always reign and sincerity and modesty will be left behind, and fortune will be the enemy of worth, and merit will not be able to make its way, and the just and the weak will be oppressed, etc., etc.

Live, Ahriman, and triumph, and you will always triumph.

Envy attributed by the ancients to the gods against men.

Animals destined for food. The serpent Boa. Merciful deity, etc.

Why, God of evil, have you put into life some semblance of pleasure? love? . . . to torment us with desire, with comparison with others, with our past, etc?

I do not know whether you love praise or blame, etc. Your praise shall be weeping, the proof of our suffering. Certainly you shall have no weeping from me: a thousand times or more your name shall be cursed by my lips, etc.

I will never resign myself, etc.

If Ahriman were ever asked a favour, etc., grant that I may never pass my 7th lustre. While I lived, I was always your greatest advocate, etc., the apostle of your religion. Reward me. I ask you nothing of what the world calls goods; I ask that which is called the greatest of evils, death (I do not ask you for riches, etc., not for love the only thing worth living for, etc.) I cannot, I cannot endure life any more.

Even though Leopardi's hymn *Ad Arimane* was not intended for use in ritual, and though it is very individual in flavour, the spirit that gave it birth is a religious one, and it must be considered as part of the tradition of the Satan cult. It belongs to the type of literary hymn which exists in every religion with priests and ritual – as far back as Babylonia, Assyria and Egypt – and is developed from cultic poetry in the narrowest sense.[10] In this poetry personal experience is always in the foreground, and often reaches the pitch of mystical possession. This is what has happened here; Leopardi's hymn is an example of Satanic mysticism. In it, the cult of Satan attains its most sublime and at the same time its most extreme form.

Leopardi gives Satan the Persian form of the Vedic name 'Angra-Mainyu'. Perhaps he does this in order to stress the fundamental nature of evil, which comes out particularly clearly in the Persian concept.

We should not get an accurate idea of the phenomenon if we were to see in Leopardi's hymn merely the result of neurotic despair, that is if we were to consider it from a purely psychological point of view. It expresses, rather, a radical metaphysical pessimism. Evil appears as the absolute basis of the world. The use of the terms 'fate', 'nature' and 'God' only serves to disguise the fact that everything in existence is a plaything for the whims of the evil creator and 'king of things'. Human evil is the medium of the divine will to evil, which uses it to destroy the ordinances and laws set up against blind caprice. Even love is powerless against the principle of evil. Every way of escape is barred. The lines about the child who at once destroys what he has made are a negative version of a fragment of Heraclitus: 'The *aion* is a child at play, moving the draughts here and there on the board; the kingship is a child's.'[11]

But the Ahriman of the hymn also has some essential features of the devouring Great Female.

Leopardi tries to overcome Christian dualism by putting in place of the *Summum Bonum* (the Highest Good), a *Summum Malum*, or Highest Evil. Thus the Satanic polemics are transformed into a pure, abysmal pessimism. The fact that the poet's prayer for an early death, expressed in the last paragraph, was fulfilled – though a few years later – shows how deeply Leopardi, who knew illness very early in life, was marked by the agony expressed in the hymn.

2 Quite a different spirit fills the hymn 'A Satana' by Giosuè Carducci (1835–1907), whose poetry earned him the Nobel Prize.[12] Carducci played an important part in Italian Freemasonry, and the following text was used as a Masonic festival song:

Giosuè Carducci, A Satana, Il popolo, Bologna, 8 December 1869 (Carducci, Opere II, pp. 577ff) (Revised edition, XXX, pp. 334ff)

To thee, immense beginning
Of existence –
Matter and spirit,
Reason and sense,

While in the chalices
The wine sparkles
Like the soul
Within the eye,

While the earth
And the sun smile,
And words of love
Are exchanged,

And there runs a shiver
Of a secret Hymen
From the mountains, and the plain
Trembles with fertility,

To thee is unleashed
The bold verse,
I call to thee, O Satan,
King of the feast.

Away with the censer,
Priest, and thy metre [i.e. chants (against Satan)]
No, priest, Satan
Turns not back!

See, the rust
Consumes Michael's
Mystical sword,
And the faithful

Archangel, his wings plucked out,
Falls into the void.
The thunderbolt is frozen
In the hand of Jehovah.

Pale meteors,
Extinguished planets,
Angels rain
From the firmaments.

In matter
That never sleeps,
King of phenomena,
King of shapes,

Alone lives Satan;
He holds the empire
In the quivering flash
Of a dark eye.

Whether languidly
He flees and resists,
Or sharp and moist
He provokes, he insists.

He shines in the joyous
Blood of the grapes,
And thus the swift
Joy does not weary,

That restores
Fleeting life,
That puts off pain
And heartens love.

Thou breathest, Satan,
In my verse,
If it bursts from my breast
Defying the god

Of the guilty Popes,
Of the bloody Kings;
And like lightning
Thou shakest the mind.

For thee, Angra-mainyu,
Adonis, Astarte,
Marble statues lived,
And paintings, and writings.

When the serene
Ionic airs
Blessed Venus
Anadyomene.

For thee the trees
Of Lebanon trembled
Who came as the lover
Of the gracious Cypris.

For thee burned
The dances and the songs,
For thee the pure
Loves of the virgins

Among the fragrant
Palms of Idumaea
Where the Cyprian foam
Gleams white,

What profits it, if barbarously
The Nazarene
Fury of the Agape
From the obscene rite

With a sacred torch
Burned thy temple
And scattered on the ground
The Argolian signs?

Thou fleddest, and the people
Among their household gods,
Remembering, received thee
In their hovels.

And then the throbbing
Heart of a woman,
Overflowing, burning,
Deity and lover,

The witch, pale
With everlasting care
Thou broughtest to succour
Sick Nature.

Thou, with the motionless eye
Of the alchemist,
Thou, with the sight
Of the untameable wizard.

Beyond the bars
Of the dull cloisters
Thou hast revealed the glittering
New heavens.

Into solitude
Fleeing from thee
In worldly things, the monk
In sadness hid.

O thou, soul divided
From thy path,
Satan is kind;
Here is Heloise.

In vain thou chastisest thyself
In harsh sackcloth.
He murmurs the verse
Of Maro [Virgil] *and Flaccus* [Horace]

Among Davidic
Dirges and weeping;
And, Delphic forms
At thy side

Rosy in the fearful
Black company
He brings Lycoris [the mistress of Cornelius Gallus, who abandoned him (see Virgil's 10th Eclogue)]
He brings Glicera [a woman celebrated by Horace]

But by other images
Of a finer age
Sometimes is populated
The sleepless cell.

From the pages
Of Livy, fiery
Tribunes, consuls,
Trembling masses

He awakens, and full of dreams
Of Italian pride
He drives thee, O monk [Arnold of Brescia (executed 1155)]
Upon the Capitol.

And you, whom the raging
Fire could not consume,
Prophetic voices,
Wyclif and Huss,

Through the air you send
The wakeful cry:
The century is renewed,
The age is complete.

And already, already tremble
Mitres and crowns;
From the cloister roars
Rebellion.

And it fights and preaches
Beneath the stole
Of Brother Girolamo
Savonarola.

Martin Luther
Threw away his cassock.
Throw away thy chains,
Human thought,

And gleam and flash
Girdled with flames;
Matter, arise;
Satan has conquered.

A beautiful and terrible
Monster is unchained.
It runs over the ocean,
Runs over the land.

Glowing and smoking
Like a volcano
It conquers the mountains,
Devours the plains.

It flies over the abysses,
Then hides itself
In unknown caverns,
In deep ways.

And emerges; and untamed
From shore to shore
Like a whirlwind
It utters its cry,

Like a whirlwind
It sends forth its breath;
There passes, O nations,
Satan the Great.

He passes, beneficent
From place to place
On the unrestrainable
Chariot of fire.

Greetings, O Satan,
O Rebellion,
O avenging power
Of reason!

May holy incense and prayers
Rise to thee!
Thou hast conquered the Jehovah
Of the priests.

Carducci's hymn is full of victorious optimism. This attitude was nourished to a considerable extent by the belief in progress which began in the Age of Enlightenment and flourished particularly in the nineteenth century. Satan becomes the symbol of the 'avenging power of reason'. This touches upon a problem that was especially acute in Italy; it is an important fact that the hymn was published only a few years after the issue of the so-called *Syllabus* of Pius IX, which severely condemned every kind of liberalism. But this is not all, for Satan is not only 'reason' but also 'sense, feeling', and there is a Dionysian passion in the verses. Finally – and here we see a dominant theme of the nineteenth century – Satan embodied the power of 'matter', which Carducci constantly relates to 'spirit'. Verse after verse opens ever newer perspectives; the hymn embraces all of pre-Christian and Christian history, and sees everywhere the spirit of Satan the Great. Carducci maintains that now – in this age – all the Messianic hopes built upon Satan are fulfilled: 'The age is complete.' The phrase recalls Jesus's words in the temple: 'This day is this scripture fulfilled in your ears.' (Luke 4: 21.) Carducci greets Satan as the Messiah, come at last. His hymn is a paean on the new-risen conqueror of God, who is the personification of servitude and unreason.

Carducci sees, in the figure of Satan, features which in classical times were an indispensable part of the image of the gods, and which Christianity attributed to the Devil. He therefore takes Satan back to his pre-diabolical essence, to which he adds certain characteristics which, in the Christian tradition, belong to the Holy Ghost (for instance, the image of the 'whirlwind'). This results in an exchange of roles; Satan becomes the *summum bonum*, the highest good, while the God of the clerics is stripped of his goodness and becomes evil. Thence the Epiphany of Satan opens amazing new perspectives. Carducci bypasses the problem of dualism as such. His optimism and his proclamation of the Messiah are possible because he passes without a glance the abyss into which Leopardi fell.

C *The Mass of Canon Docre in J. K. Huysmans Là-bas*

Joris Karl Huysmans (1848–1907)[13] turned from literary naturalism around the year 1885, and began an intensive study of occultism and magic, which had become fashionable at the time. He held spiritualist seances in his flat, and soon became interested in Satanism. In 1889, when seeking material for his novel *Là-bas*, he met a lady who told him about the priest who became the model for his Canon Docre. Huysmans then met the excommunicated Abbé Boullan, who lived in Lyons. Boullan believed himself to be the successor of the mystic and prophet Eugène Vintras, who died in Lyons in 1875; according to stories told in occultist circles, many parapsychological phenomena had taken place in Vintras's presence. Boullan (who appears in *Là-bas* as Doctor Johannes) was in conflict with Stanislas de Guaita, the Rosicrucian leader. He entered into a detailed correspondence with

Huysmans, and gave him the information he wanted. In one of his letters he says:

> Satanism is much more prevalent among the clergy than you could ever suspect. I will give you the opportunity to convince yourself of this. For I must emphasise that Satanism today is more learned and cultured than it was in the Middle Ages; it is practised in Rome as well as in France, particularly Paris, Lyons and Châlons, and in Belgium, in Bruges.[14]

Huysmans took Boullan's side in the conflict with the Rosicrucians, in which parapsychological phenomena also played a large part. He shared in Lyons in the Abbé's rite known as the 'communion of Melchizedek'.

Huysmans was without a doubt also present at least once at one of the actual black masses which were held regularly in the neighbourhood of his flat (Rue de Sèvres).[15] He obtained supplementary details for his description of the black mass from documents in the Vintras archives and the records of the trial of the possessed prophetess Cantianille.

Huysmans was deeply fascinated by Satanism. Only thus can we explain the poetic form of the prayers and blasphemies he puts into the mouth of Canon Docre. These extracts form the substance of his picture of the black mass.

At the beginning of 1891 *Là-bas* appeared in the *Echo de Paris* prior to publication. Two years later Abbé Boullan died. His sudden death was attributed to sympathetic magic on the part of de Guaita. Huysmans came into possession of consecrated wafers which Boullan had used in his cult. Some had congealed blood on them; others bore, besides the cross, cabbalistic signs.

Huysmans took under his protection Madame Thibault, whom Vintras had ordained priestess of the 'Church of Elias-Carmel' and who was considered a prophetess and saint. Since, after Boullan's death, he felt that he himself was exposed to the attacks of de Guaita, he had Madame Thibault perform protective rites every day. Finally de Guaita died (his death too was attributed to magic) and Huysmans could live in peace again. At this time he began to turn with extraordinary intensity to the Catholic faith. He was converted, and his novel *En route*, published in 1895, was a record of his final return to the Church.

A Host, consecrated by Vintras, used by Abbe Boullan.

And now the description of the black mass from *Là-bas*:

Joris Karl Huysmans, Là-bas (1st edition Paris 1891). From ch. XIX, 23rd edn, Paris 1904, pp. 368ff.

They were in a chapel with a low ceiling crossed by roughly tarred beams, windows hidden by heavy curtains, and cracked, faded walls. Durtal recoiled after the first few steps. Heating vents blew out whirls of steam; a horrible smell of damp, mustiness, and a new stove, aggravated by the pungent odour of potash, resin and burning herbs, caught at his throat and pressed on his temples.

He groped his way forward, peering into the depths of the chapel, which was dimly lit by sanctuary lamps suspended from the ceiling in gilded bronze and pink glass holders . . . Durtal noticed that among those present there were very few men and many women. . . .

A choirboy dressed in red walked to the far end of the chapel and lit a row of candles. Then the altar appeared, an ordinary church altar surmounted by a tabernacle, and, above that, an infamous caricature of Christ. His head had been raised and his neck elongated, and the lines painted on his cheeks transformed his tragic face into a mask twisted into a horrible smile. He was naked, and instead of the loincloth, man's most ignoble member protruded, erect, from a bush of hair. In front of the tabernacle, a chalice with its cover was placed; the choirboy smoothed the altar cloth with his hands, wriggled his hips, stood on one foot as though to fly away, and played at being a cherub on the pretext of trying to reach the black candles whose odour of bitumen and pitch had now joined the noisome half-stifled smells of this room. . . .

Then another choirboy, uglier still, showed himself. Skinny, hollow-cheeked with coughing, his complexion repaired with white and carmine grease-paint. He hobbled in, humming to himself. He went up to the tripods on each side of the altar, stirred up the embers lying among the ashes, and threw on pieces of resin and leaves. . . .

'Then are we in a real chapel?' he [Durtal] asked.

'Yes, this house, this church, this garden we passed through, are the remains of an old Ursuline convent, now in ruins.'

'But what are they burning for it to stink like that?'

'Rue, leaves of henbane and thorn-apple, dried nightshades and myrrh; they are perfumes pleasing to Satan, our master!' . . .

Preceded by the two choirboys and wearing a scarlet cap adorned with two bison's horns of red material, the Canon entered.

Durtal looked at him closely as he walked to the altar. He was tall but awkwardly built, deep-chested; his hairless forehead dropped without a curve into a straight nose; his lips and cheeks bristled with those hard thick hairs seen on old priests after long shaving; his features were coarse and sinuous, his eyes, like apple-pips, small, black, close to the nose, shone in the dark. In all, his physiognomy was ugly and ravaged, but full of energy. . . .

He bowed solemnly in front of the altar, walked up the steps and began his Mass.

Durtal then saw that under his vestments he was naked. His flesh, pushed down by garters fastened high, appeared above his black socks. His chasuble was the normal shape of chasubles, but was the dark red of dried blood, and in the centre, in a triangle surrounded by a vegetation of meadow-saffron, savin, wine-apples and spurge, a black he-goat stood with horns pointing forward.

Docre genuflected and made slight or deep bows as the ritual demanded; the choirboys, kneeling, gave the Latin responses in a crystal-clear voice with a singing lilt at the ends of the words.

'Yes, but that's an ordinary low mass,' said Durtal to Mme Chantelouve.

She shook her head. And in fact, at that moment the choirboys went behind the altar, and reappeared, one carrying copper braziers and the other censers which they distributed to those present. All the women wrapped themselves in clouds of smoke; some flung themselves down with their heads above the braziers, drawing the scent into both nostrils, then, fainting, they loosened their dresses, gasping harshly.

Then the Mass was interrupted. The Priest came backwards down the steps, knelt on the bottom one, and in a shrill trembling voice he cried:

'Master of Scandals, Distributor of the benefits of crime, Steward of magnificent sins and great vices, Satan, it is you we worship, logical God, just God!

More than admirable legate of false fears, you accept our mendicant tears; you save the honour of our families by aborting wombs that have conceived in forgetful moments of joyous crisis; you sow in the hearts of mothers the haste to miscarry; and like a kind midwife you take away the anguish of maturity, the pain of falls, from children who die before they are born!

Support of the embittered poor, Restorer of the vanquished, you bestow on them hypocrisy, ingratitude, conceit, that they may defend themselves against the attacks of the children of God, the rich!

Sovereign of contempt, Book-keeper of humiliations, Lessee of old hates, you alone fertilise the brain of the man crushed by injustice; you whisper to him ideas of premeditated vengeance, of infallible misdeeds; you incite him to murders, you give him the exuberant joy of reprisals achieved, the pleasant intoxication of tortures accomplished, of tears he has caused!

Hope of manhoods, anguish of empty wombs, Satan, you do not ask for vain proofs of chaste loins, you do not boast of the madness of fasts and rest days, you alone receive the supplications of the flesh and the little notes for poor and covetous families. You decide the mother to sell her daughter, to give up her son, you help sterile and reprobate loves, Guardian of strident Neuroses, leaden Tower of Hysterias, bloody Vessel of Rapes:

Master, your faithful servants implore you, kneeling. They beg you to give them the joy of those delightful crimes unknown to justice; they beg you to help the misdeeds whose unknown traces confuse man's reason; they beg you to hear them when they ask for the torture of all who love and serve them. Finally they pray for glory, riches, power, to you, King of the disinherited, the Son banished by the inexorable Father!'

Then Docre rose, and standing with outstretched arms, he shouted in a voice clear and full of hate:

'And you, you whom in my capacity as priest I force, whether you will or not, to come down into this host, to become incarnate in this bread, Jesus, Craftsman of deceptions, Thief of homage, Robber of affections, hear me! From the day you came forth an ambassador from the womb of a Virgin, you have broken your contracts, gone back on your promises; centuries have waited sobbing for you, dumb, elusive God! You were to have redeemed man, and you have redeemed nothing; you were to have appeared in your sleep! Go, tell your lies, say to the wretch who calls you: "Hope, be patient, suffer; the hospice of souls will receive you, the angels will assist you, Heaven is opening." Impostor! You well know that the angels are departing, disgusted with your inertia! You should have been the Mediator of our complaints, the Chamberlain of our tears, you should have brought them before the Father, and you have not done it, because doubtless this intercession would have disturbed your sleep in a smug, sated Eternity!

You have forgotten the Poverty you preached, Vassal in love with Banks! You have seen the weak crushed beneath the press of the premium, you have heard the gasps of the timid crippled by famine, of women disembowelled for a little bread, and through the Chancellery of your Simoniacs, through your commercial representatives, through your Popes, you replied with dilatory excuses, evasive promises, Lawyer of the sacristy, God of business!

Monster whose inconceivable ferocity engendered life and inflicted it on innocents whom you dare to condemn, in the name of who knows what original sin, whom you dare to punish, in virtue of who knows what clauses, we long nevertheless to make you admit at last your impudent lies, your inexpiable crimes! We long to hammer in your nails, press on your thorns, bring back the painful blood to the lips of your dried wounds!

And this we can and will do, violating the quest of your Body, Profaner of great vices, Fabricator of stupid purity, accursed Nazarene, sluggard King, coward God!'

'Amen,' cried the crystal voices of the choirboys.

Durtal listened to this torrent of blasphemies and insults; the filthy mind of this priest stupefied him; Silence followed these howlings; the chapel was filled with the smoke of the censers. The women, who up to now had said nothing, became excited when the Canon, going back to the altar, turned and blessed them with a sweeping gesture of his left hand.

And suddenly the choirboys rang little bells.

It was like a signal. Women fell on to the carpet and rolled there. One seemed to be moved by a spring; she threw herself on her belly and sawed the air with her feet. Another, suddenly struck by a hideous squint, yelped, then lost her voice and lay with her jaw dropped and her tongue retracted with the tip turned up against the palate; another, swollen, livid, her pupils dilated, threw back her head on her shoulders, then straightened it with a sudden jerk, and, gasping, ploughed down her throat with her nails; yet another, lying on her back, unfastened her skirt, brought out an enormous, distended, naked belly, then twisted herself in horrible grimaces, and stuck out, without being able to put it back, a white tongue with ragged edges, from a mouth full of blood, with a portcullis of red teeth.

At once Durtal stood up to see better, and he distinctly heard and saw Canon Docre.

He was gazing at the figure of Christ above the tabernacle, and, with arms outstretched, was vomiting forth appalling indecencies, screaming, with every ounce of his strength, insults worthy of a drunken cabman. One of the choirboys knelt before him, turning his back to the altar. A shiver ran down the priest's spine. In a solemn tone but a trembling voice he said: 'Hoc est enim corpus meum,' then, instead of kneeling, after the consecration, before the precious Body, he turned to the congregation a swollen, haggard face, streaming with sweat.

He staggered between the two choirboys who lifted the chasuble to show his naked belly, and held it while the host, which he carried in front of him, fell, damaged and soiled, on to the steps.

Then Durtal felt himself shudder, for a wind of madness shook the room. An aura of extreme hysteria followed the sacrilege and flung the women to the ground; while the choirboys bathed the naked priest in incense, women rushed for the Eucharistic Bread, and, prone at the foot of the altar, clawed at it, tore off damp crumbs, ate and drank this divine ordure.

Another, crouched on a crucifix, burst into heart-rending laughter, then cried out 'My priest, my priest!'; an old woman tore out her hair, leapt, pirouetted, bent down, stood on one foot, and collapsed beside a girl who, pressed against a wall, jerked in convulsions, foamed at the mouth, and, weeping, spat out appalling blasphemies. And Durtal, horrified, saw in the smoke, as though through a fog, the red horns of Docre, who, seated now, was slavering with rage, chewing the unleavened bread, spitting it out again, wiping himself with it and distributing it to the women; they engulfed it, howling, or fell over each other to violate it.

It was a raging madhouse cell, a monstrous sweat-room full of harlots and lunatics. Then, while the choirboys joined the men, and the lady of the house climbed on to the altar with her skirts tucked up, seized the Christ-figure's member with one hand, and with the other pushed the chalice between her naked legs, at the far end of the chapel, in the shadows, a little girl, who had not yet moved, suddenly bent forward and howled like a dog!

Sick with disgust and half suffocated, Durtal longed to escape. He looked for Hyacinthe, but she was no longer there. He saw her at last beside the Canon. He stepped over bodies intertwined on the carpet and went up to her. With quivering nostrils, she was breathing in the odours of incense and copulation.

'The smell of the Sabbath!' she whispered to him through clenched teeth.

'Now then – are you coming at last?'

She seemed to wake up, hesitated a moment, then, without replying, followed him.

He elbowed his way out, shaking off the women who were now showing their teeth, ready to bite. He pushed Mme Chantelouve towards the door, passed through the courtyard and the vestibule, and, as the porter's lodge was empty, he pulled the door-string and found himself in the street.

Mme Chantelouve and Durtal go into a nearby café. The proprietor takes them into a room in his house.

'I want you,' she said; and she won him traitorously, forcing him to desire it.

And she undressed and threw her dress and petticoats on the floor, opened wide the horrible bed, and, lifting up her shift, she rubbed her spine against the harsh stuff of the sheets, her eyes misty, laughing with delight!

She grabbed him and showed him prisoners' tricks, infamies of which he had never even suspected her; she seasoned them with ghoulish fury, and suddenly, when he managed to escape, he shuddered, for in the bed he saw fragments of the host.

Canon Docre's Mass takes place in the chapel of a former Ursuline convent, probably because the places of residence of this particular order acquired a special importance in the history of the Satan cult, especially where cases of possession were concerned (see above, p. 99f).

In crude contrast to the Church's representation of Christ crucified, a caricature has been set up over the altar. In the Gospels Christ is never described as laughing, but here his face is set in a 'horrible smile' (cf. Plate 4). The Christ of ecclesiastical tradition is asexual; but here he appears as ithyphallic (with erect penis). In classical times the ithyphallus played an important part as a symbol of fertility and ecstasy, both with the god Pan and his father (or son) Priapus[16] and in the cult of Dionysus.[17] In Christianity the area symbolised by the ithyphallus was largely considered as belonging to the Devil, so that the ithyphallic symbol itself came to be considered obscene. The special significance of the ithyphallic Christ is shown by a passage from an essay by Huysmans on the erotic work of Rops: 'Basically . . . nobody is quite as obscene as a chaste person. In fact everyone knows that continenence produces most unbridled thoughts.'[18] The fact that not Satan but Christ is given crude sexual characteristics means not only a reawakening of pre-Christian elements – taking a distorted form in Satanism – but at the same time an attempt to unmask the Christian idea, concentrated in the figure of Christ; that is to say, the 'unbridled thoughts' of the pure and chaste Christian are brought to light in the very model of purity.

The focal point of the black mass as described by Huysmans consists of the two poetically worded invocations – the prayer to Satan and the diatribe against Christ. The orations are in the form of extended litanies, and correspond to the Preface and in part to the Canon of the Roman Mass.

The prayer to Satan is very similar in content to Baudelaire's 'Litanies de Satan', except that here the basic mood is different, and everything is expressed in a much more impulsive and extreme way. In Huysmans too there is a note of social criticism; Satan is the king of the poor and weak, those driven to crime, the social and moral outcasts. He is called 'logical God, just God', because he holds the torch of ethical and social equality for all men. The insults hurled at the crucifix have a certain similarity with the Grand Inquisitor's reproaches to Christ in Dostoevsky's *Brothers Karamazov*: '. . . Dost thou care only for the tens of thousands of the great and strong, while the millions, numerous as the sands of the sea, who are weak but love thee, must exist only for the sake of the great and strong?. . . . And besides, how many of those elect, those mighty ones who could become elect, have grown weary waiting for thee . . .'[19]

Even though the Grand Inquisitor does not mean those in material and social power by his 'elect' and 'strong', and even though the central theme of his reproaches is not – as here – the identification of God with the rich, but the imposition of an intolerable freedom, there is still at a certain point a correspondence between the words of the Grand Inquisitor and those of Canon Docre; God is a god of the 'aristocracy'; he ignores the needs of the masses and makes impossible demands on normal men. The blasphemies put into Docre's mouth are an extreme reaction to the continual excessive demands of an ideal of spiritual perfection unattainable by the common people, and even more unacceptable because – and this was particularly true of nineteenth-century bourgeois Christianity – it was used to prop up social barriers. The desire to drive in the nails and the crown of thorns even deeper, and the defilement of the consecrated Host recall the *Histoire véritable* of 1623 (see above, p. 89).

The hysterical fits of the women present are vividly described.

In the nineteenth century, a time of particularly strong collective sexual repression, attacks of this kind, known as *grande hystérie*[20] were very characteristic.

To complete the picture, we quote a few more details which Huysmans gives on the basis of his researches in Satanism for *Là-bas*:

> In 1855 a society arose in Paris, composed for the greater part of women. These women took communion several times a day, kept the sacred wafer in their mouths and later spat it out in order to tear it up or soil it by objectionable means. . . . I may also mention that in 1874 women were appointed in Paris to carry on this detestable business; they were paid by the piece, which may explain whey they were to be found day after day at the Holy Table in various churches. . . . This is a periodical issued in 1843, *La Voix de la Semaine*. It tells us that a Satanist society in Agen celebrated black masses uninterruptedly for twenty-five years, and destroyed and defiled three thousand, three hundred and twenty hosts.[21]

Nineteenth-century Satanism, the result of mysticism in protest against positivism, and practised by 'decadents' steeped in romantic ideas of religion, produced no ritual practices that were not known in earlier times; its originality lies exclusively in what we have called the 'romantic style' of the Satan cult.

8 EPIGONAL PHENOMENA AND SURREALIST ALIENATION OF THE SATAN CULT IN THE TWENTIETH CENTURY

We have seen that the nineteenth century added no new ritual elements to the Satan cult; and, in the twentieth century too, the actual black mass was completely epigonal in character. But at the same time a kind of ironic detachment led to new possibilities, influenced particularly by surrealism.

A *Satires on the Christian religion by the early Bolsheviks: a fringe phenomenon*

René Fülöp-Miller, in his work *Geist und Gesicht des Bolschewismus*, showed that the basic ideas of Bolshevism are closely connected with the notions of redemption of a series of Russian sects which had in common the belief in a Kingdom of God to be fulfilled in this world – that is to say an earthly paradise – and the ideal of poverty and of struggle against the rule of Church and Society.[1] The author divides these sects into two groups: the rational-ethical and the mystic-orgiastic. The most important of the latter group are the 'Chlysti' (whippers) and the sect, derived from them, of 'Skopzen' (eunuchs). The rites of the two sects, which have opposite attitudes towards sex, interest us insofar as they contain elements related to the Satan cult. Füllöp-Miller describes a typical religious festival of the Chlysti, based in Central Russia, and particularly in the Moscow region:

> In a building specially chosen for the purpose, or even if necessary in a barn, there is set up in the middle of the meeting-room a barrel of water, which is supposed to be a symbol of the River Jordan. All those present, men and women, strip to the skin, seize green twigs which are kept in readiness, and begin to whip, first the water in the barrel, then each other, until they go into an ecstasy. . . . When their continued flagellation has thrown them into a state of ever-increasing excitement, they go on to the wildest orgies, in which complete promiscuity reigns, except for one couple, chosen for the procreation of the Child of God. These two . . . must not embrace until the general

> ecstasy has reached its zenith. During the whole of the festival, which is supposed to lead finally to an appearance of the Holy Ghost, dances go on constantly, working up to a state of trance.[2]

Rasputin, the 'dancing *Staretz*', who arranged orgiastic festivals, was decisively influenced by the Chlysti.[3] The Skopzen too, who considered the 'Royal Seal' (self-mutilation, that is castration for men and removal of the breasts for women – an interpretation of Matth. 19: 12, Luke 33: 29, and Rev. 7: 2ff.) as essential to salvation, indulged in wild dances of the Dervish type. There are obvious parallels with phenomena we have already described.

In the early days of Bolshevism there was also something like an erotic and orgiastic cult – the wild festivals, called 'African nights', of the Komsomol, an atheistic youth movement.[4] Here too the rites of the orthodox Church were caricatured. Füllöp-Miller gives us the facts:

> Festivals were organised which ran parallel to the ecclesiastical institutions which had hitherto been customary. Thus in the towns, at Christmas, Easter and Whitsuntide, antireligious Christmas, Easter and Whitsuntide festivals were held in front of the churches. On such occasions the 'priest' appeared in a dress which caricatured the actual vestments of a priest, and was supposed to amuse the godless company. A 'red prayer' was said, and a 'red Mass' held, both intended as parodies of the rites of the Orthodox Church. Finally the choir sang well-known hymns, with the words altered to a disgusting mockery of Christ, the Mother of God and the saints. Sometimes even the melodies were degraded by the unexpected insertion of a few bars of a revolutionary song or even an obscene street ballad. Instead of pictures of the saints they used either caricatures of godly personages or portraits of Communist leaders. Similar pictures and painted banners were also carried in procession through the streets by atheistic 'acolytes', together with large puppet-heads representing God the Father, Christ, Buddha and Allah. At the end of a mock procession of this sort, the street urchins, at the command of the 'priest', spat on these puppets, whipped them, broke them up, or publicly burnt them. Many of these mock processions were turned into great festivals, with the collaboration of the most famous poets,

painters and theatrical producers. Among such productions are the 'Godless Mystery of the Birth of Komsomol (the Godless)' and the satirical mystery 'The non-Immaculate Conception' by Tretiakov.[5]

We may also mention in this context the mock icons (Plate 3). In order to realise their importance, we must consider the part played by icons in the Orthodox Church, as respositories of divine power, as tangible representations of the Intangible, and as cult objects.[6]

An essential feature of these phenomena in the early days of Bolshevism is that the participants no longer identify themselves absolutely with their antichristian utterances, as has been hitherto the case in the history of the Satan cult, but maintain a certain, definitely ironic, detachment. This is also expressed in the fact that a commentary on the mock rituals was often given by a comic figure. This 'alienation effect' combines with an element of surrealism – in the broadest sense – which is particularly evident in the icon on the Marriage in Cana; paradoxical elements are juxtaposed to bring out a latent meaning.

It has often been justly emphasised that Bolshevism and Communism were based on religious conviction[7] secularised and disguised as science. This stems from the idea of an earthly paradise, based on the one hand (as Füllop-Miller shows) on the redemption beliefs of Russian sects, and on the other hand on the Utopias of Western religious writers, particularly those of Thomas More and Thomas Campanella,[8] which were well known and often quoted by Communist writers from Marx to Lenin. But the conception of Paradise is evolved from materialism, from which Communist doctrine and practice in general are derived.

Unlike the religions of antiquity, in which the material and the spiritual are in dynamic equilibrium, Christianity overemphasises the spiritual principle and the male patriarchal element that goes with it. Materialism – that is, the elevation of matter to the highest principle – must be seen as a reaction to it, and it is no accident that Marx followed directly after Hegel, who carried the Christian attitude to the point of proclaiming the absolute nature of the spirit. Both phenomenologically and etymologically, 'matter' is connected with *mater* – mother – thus expressing one aspect of the Great Female principle. Materialism is a revolution against the patriarchal Christian concentration on the spirit (Carducci too says 'Matter, rise'.) Much the same applies to the Communist expectation of Paradise; it is a reaction against a one-sided spiritual belief in the Beyond, which did not exist in antiquity either. The earthly paradise is, as it were, set up in opposition to the kingdom of the Heavenly Father, and is the domain of a universally bountiful female element. In his book *Psychoanalyse und Sociologie*, Aurel Kolnai says: 'The proletariat, shut out from the earth, longs, as its one aim in life, to return to it . . . dreams . . . of the Paradise of the Earth-mother. 'Kind Mother Nature has allowed for everything', as W. Weitling says. The anarchic and communistic attitude is, as we know, a regression to the mother.[9] Since the negative, devouring side of the female principle is assimilated with the positive, nourishing side, there arises at the same time a system of collectivistic pressures with its attendant threat to individuality.

Caricatures of the Christian religion and religious pictures in the early days of Bolshevism (later the phenomenon ceased to exist) support the convictions we have outlined. From the point of view of religious phenomenology, they can be seen both as an attempt to unmask Christian attitudes (see above, p. 141) and as anti-spiritual polemics.

B *Satanic phenomena in Anglo-Saxon, Germanic, and Romance-speaking countries*

Great Britain and Australia

Great Britain, a country that has a particularly rich tradition in the history of the witch cult,[10] has not so far provided any of the documents quoted in our study. This is because it was not 'creative' in the field of the actual Satan cult. In the twentieth century, England, and especially London, has become a centre for the black mass, but all the phenomena concerned are derivative.

One of the most outstanding figures of the more recent occult sciences is the Englishman Aleister Crowley (1875–1947),[11] who, quoting from the Apocalypse, called himself *To Mega Therion* (the Great Beast). Crowley left the Hermetic order of the Golden Dawn and founded the *Ordo Argentinum Astrum* and the *Abbey of Thelema* (derived from Rabelais's *Gargantua*), which had a few imitations with the same name. Besides numerous essays and poems he composed a Gnostic form of Mass.[12] The ritual, the style of which shows a strong art nouveau influence, was taken as a black mass by some groups of his followers, particularly in North America.

(I should like to take this opportunity of pointing out that I cannot here go into the relationships between the practice of the Satan cult or its fringe phenomena and the modern secret societies such as the Freemasons, which are particularly prevalent in Great Britain and Italy. In the first place these relationships are so complex that they are almost incomprehensible to outsiders; and in the second place random samples show that they do not provide any new material for our phenomenological study.)

Two items chosen at random from the Press may shed some light on present-day Satan worship in Great Britain:

> The former Detective-Superintendent Robert Fabian of Scotland Yard has established that regular devilworship with prescribed rites is carried on in various places in the heart of London, and that the number of its adherents is increasing. 'Black masses', accompanied by the burning of aromatic herbs, are held by candlelight in front of an altar hung with black and marked with signs of the Zodiac; they are often followed by sexual orgies. The *Church Times*, a serious periodical, even claims to know that unfrocked priests occasionally take part, and consecrate bread and wine at the black masses. A number of men and women of high intelligence and well-known names are said to be among the followers of this cult. . . . Obscene ceremonies, blood-sacrifices of animals, and ritual dances to throbbing drums are all said to be quite usual.[13]

> The British police are at present concerned with Devil worshippers who steal vestments and silver from churches to use in black masses. As a result of the constantly increasing number of thefts from churches, the Yorkshire County Constabulary were obliged to appeal to the clergy and Church officers to take special precautions for the safety of vestments and silver, and most especially of communion chalices. Several churches in Yorkshire have been robbed by Devil worshippers. On the advice of the police, many churches which are normally kept open in the daytime have now been locked to prevent their

desecration by 'black masses'. Vestments, silver vessels and a bottle of Communion wine have been stolen from the parish church of Smeaton, near Pontefract. Edmund Barret, Vicar of Smeaton, said: 'We believe that the thieves intend to use their booty for black magic, since they only took certain objects and left behind others which are far more valuable. An ordinary thief would have taken much more silver instead of my vestments and the Communion wine.'[14]

The periodical *Life* also carried a long, profusely illustrated report on witchcraft and the Satan cult in present-day Great Britain.[15] In the Witchcraft Museum at Bourton-on-the-Water there is an altar with a wax figure intended to illustrate this type of ritual.

It is remarkable how many of those taking part in Satanic rites are upper-class intellectuals. The reason is probably that people who are particularly cut off from popular and primitive sources of vitality are seeking to gain experiences of an elemental kind in the Satan cult and the orgies connected with it. Here too the compensatory nature of the black mass is obvious; the Apollonian, spiritual religion of the Church and the empty, conventional quasireligious institutions of our culture cannot satisfy this need. The essential thing is the search for collective experiences, which are expected to bring liberation from the barren waste land of isolation. The following example comes from Australia:

In Sydney, the 37-year-old painter Rosaleen Norton celebrated Black Masses in her flat. The participants were men and women who were unhappy in love. After the devil-worship came unbridled orgies. . . . The altar was dedicated to Satan, and the Black Masses were celebrated kneeling before it. A skull was passed from hand to hand among those present. A 'Devil's priest' parodied the Lord's Prayer and poured out Scotch whisky as communion wine.[16]

The old black magic tradition of love spells shows that those unfortunate in love tended to seek the help of the Devil; but here it appears as though the only purpose were to compensate for lost love (in psychoanalytical terms, frustration results in regression). The skull is a symbol of the Underworld as Satan's kingdom.

France

As with other countries, we can give only a few characteristic phenomena from twentieth-century France.[17]

December 1903 saw the publication of a special number of the Paris-based periodical *L'assiette au beurrė*, devoted to the black mass. The text accompanying the jacket design is as follows:

A host of sickly equivocal youths
Excitedly waits for the Prince of Demons.
They say: 'Come to us, Master whom we love,
Our lips beg you and our arms call you.'

On the nerveless body of some young woman,
Anxious, too, for the infernal lover,
The Black Mass is about slowly to unfold
Its stupid responses and infamous rites.

But the Archangel [i.e. Satan] *is doubtless visiting*
Many other strange sad imbeciles.
He declines to enter their house,
And has kept them waiting for several nights.

The decadence of the contemporary Satan cult is handled here with obvious irony.

The Satan-figure over the altar for the black mass on the dust-jacket of *Messes Noires* by Jehan Sylvius, published in 1909, corresponds to Eliphas Lévi's famous image:[18] Satan has one arm pointing upwards, the other downwards. In occultism this attitude is very significant; it is the same as that of the joker in the tarot pack, which is also related to the symbolism of *Aleph*, the first letter in the Hebrew alphabet.[19] The fact that he is pointing upwards and downwards at the same time signifies the correspondence between above and below in the cosmos, and thus the perfect unity of the world. Since *Aleph*, like the joker, is a symbol of Jehovah, Satan in this position becomes the principle of the unity of all things and the origin of the universe, that is to say he is put in the place of God.

Motifs from the Satan cult or its fringe phenomena appear constantly in the Surrealist movement in France. Without identifying themselves with the objects, the artists make Satanic or near-Satanic 'visual puns' in their paintings. In a collage Max

Ernst has a naked woman in front of a Pope who is walking in solemn procession into St Peter's Cathedral, with a man drinking in the foreground – a symbolism which needs no explanation after what has already been said in this book. On Clovis Trouille, whose painting 'Mon Caveau' we reproduce (Plate 4). Marcel Jean says:

> Trouille loves . . . the extravagance and the magnificent ornament of Catholic vestments, and sees in the ceremonious dressing-up a kind of equivocal magic, related in his mind to the secular attraction of feminine underwear. His nuns are harlots at the same time, and his monks are gay dogs in the best tradition of primitive anticlericalism. . . . The strait-laced pious sisters and priests, maddened by seductive courtesans, the glorious women constantly offering their lovely bodies, have a fantastic and often deeply moving charm.[20]

Even though sado-masochistic elements predominate in this picture, it has a gentle touch of humour throughout. The laughing Christ, the combination of the monstrance and the chamber-pot, the fusion of a macabre graveyard atmosphere with the cult of the sensual are all variations on Satanic themes.

a b c d

Erotic Church Sculpture:
a) Ornament from Raffael's room in the Vatican
b) From the Schottenkirche, Regensburg.
c) and d) From the Bishop's Palace in Sens.

Italy

The Cardinal of Milan writes in a pastoral letter: 'There are isolated organised groups who attempt to gain possession of consecrated hosts, which they desecrate and use at their meetings for unspeakable purposes.' In another letter, the same Church leader writes: 'A sect is at work, playing the part of Judas the traitor; it is all the more reprehensible because of their abuse of children.' We may assume that the stolen hosts are used in the black mass.[21]

In January 1963, in the Teatro Laboratorio in the Trastevere district of Rome, the dress rehearsal was held of the play *Cristo 63* by Carmelo Bene, produced by the author.[22] It was a parody of the story of the Passion. Even before the first night the police banned it for obscenity and sacrilege. Christ appears in the play as a drunken docker, Mary Magdalene as a whore and the apostles as an underworld gang or as clowns. During the action the performers strip completely, and one of them relieves himself on stage. The Last Supper is a drunken feast with spaghetti and chianti. All this is obviously connected with the Satan cult.

Spain

Another surrealistic form of Satan-cult motifs appears in the Last Supper scene from Luis Buñuel's film *Viridiana*.[23] A group of beggars is gathered round a table, and for one moment of stillness the picture is exactly that of Leonardo da Vinci's *Last Supper*. After a cock has crowed three times, a woman pulls her skirts over her head, to photograph the scene, as she says, 'with the camera I had from my parents'.[24] During the orgy that follows, the Hallelujah Chorus from Handel's *Messiah* is heard. This sequence is not at all like Carmelo Bene's play. Buñuel has declared in so many words that in his film, which is full of profane allusions to the Gospels, he had absolutely no blasphemous intent: 'I put in these pitiless images quite at random. If I had been pious, I should perhaps have used them just the same.'[25] Although a section of the public and the Press (the *Osservatore Romano*, for example) had a different idea of the film, we cannot doubt its creator's word. Luis Buñuel, who once said in an interview that his religious upbringing and surrealism had both had a decisive influence on his life, is not trying to advance a thesis, merely to oppose 'the withering away of the primeval life-force to cultural and ideological "values" '.[26]

Brazil

The Macumba snake rites of Brazil recall the snake cult of the Ophites (see above, p. 32ff). The women form a magic circle round a snake as it emerges from its cage (cf. p. 35 above). As with Candomblé, Xango and other Brazilian cults, Macumba combines ritual elements from Africa (which came with the Negro slaves) with parts of Indian mysteries and Christian features.[27] There is also an ecstatic eruption of primitive Dionysian forces for which there is no place in a Christian society. Werner Kemper says from his own observation: 'The European, directly confronted with this utterly different world of experience, in which all frontiers appear to vanish, is shattered to feel how relative his traditional, absolute standards really are. The melting-pot of Brazil seems to seethe with an overwhelming, bewildering abundance of irresistible forces.'[28]

Germany

In an important North German weekly, which has to be taken seriously, a Herr von B. tells of an 'adventure' he had in Frankfurt-am-Main. He had just got out of the train in Frankfurt Central Station, when someone suddenly put a piece of paper into his coat pocket. On it was a black skull with a red diagonal cross over it, and underneath were the words: 'Do you want to meet the ruler of this world? Come to this place tonight. A black limousine will be waiting for you. The great brothers of the Black Spirit.' Herr von B. went, and really was picked up in a black Mercedes and taken to a suburb. There he was blindfolded and led for a short distance, taken into a house and down some steps, and then his blindfold was removed. The following scene met his eyes: In a room hung with tapestries and other wall-hangings, in a green half-light, there were about fifty cloaked figures, conversing in whispers. On an altar in the foreground were two red-streaked human skulls, symbols of the power of Hell. A muted gong was heard, and the priest of the sect came in. The fanatics fell on their knees before him, and did not get up until the leader of the sect had censed them with sulphur-smoke. Then the newcomer had to drink the 'immunising potion' so as not to be poisoned by 'Satan's brew'. 'Here you must take this chalice with wine from Purgatory,' said the leader of the sect to him, 'and with this blade open the vein at the tip of your right thumb. Three drops of blood in the wine, and all is well.' 'And all is well,' murmured the crowd of believers, which included ten women. The religious ceremony reached its height when the leader of the sect fell into an ecstasy to the monotonous chanting of blasphemous songs by the whole company. 'The Black Spirit will annihilate the world. Satan's brew is in our hands, a handful will poison the whole world. We dedicate our heart and our faith to the Devil.' After that, curses were uttered against everything on earth, sacred and secular. And a deep genuflection to Satan ended the religious ceremony, celebrated at Frankfurt-am-Main in June 1950.[29]

It is most unusual for a complete stranger to be introduced into a circle of this kind, for, of course, considerable difficulties could be expected if the affair were to become known. It all gives a very theatrical impression. The 'Satan's brew' is considered to be a mana-containing substance, so powerful that an 'immunising potion' (a well-known motif from the history of magic[30]) had to be administered. However, the report appears to be distorted by some interpretative embroidery. It is not very probable that the whole world, 'sacred and secular', should be cursed and threatened with extinction. In fact Satan almost always represents a definitely 'secular' principle, but if Satanism coincides with absolute pessimism (as it did with Leopardi) it does not lead to sentimental and theatrical cult-forms, nor to ritual of an ecstatic type.

Austria

Finally we will look at two phenomena, very similar to each other, from Austria. These are the 'material' or 'action' theatre productions of the Viennese *avant-garde* directors Otto Mühl and Hermann Nitsch.

The following text is by Otto Mühl. It is the description of his 'action': *Kreuzigung* (Crucifixion)

I

I place a heavy wooden cross against the wall and fix it there. A male model gets up on to the podium in front of the cross so that he can touch the horizontal beam with outstretched arms. I bind his hands and feet with cords to the cross.

I daub the body with black, red, white and yellow paint and sludge.

I throw flour, egg-yolk, thick gelatinous gluten paste, sugar and breadcrumbs on to the body.

I bind the body more tightly to the cross with rags dipped in paint. Meanwhile it is constantly bespattered with paint and food.

I throw a tangled mass of ropes on to the model's head.

I stuff ropes under the rags in front of the belly so that they look like guts hanging out.

I smear a thick yellow substance like pus under the ropes and the rags.

I throw white paint on to the ropes and into the 'crown of thorns'.

I throw black powder-paint on to the figure with my hands, so that the victim disappears behind a black cloud.

Then I fling bright red paint on to the body and rags together. I tug, tear and haul on the rags, knot and entangle them more.

I take a thick rope and wrap it in a spiral round cross and body. Meanwhile I make huge knots in the rope and carry it over and under the rags.

Finally I throw black powder-paint again over the whole structure and obliterate it utterly.

2

At a sign from me, a fat woman takes her place on the podium before the wooden cross fixed to the wall.

I sign to her to raise her arms sideways to a horizontal position.

I bind her in this position on to the wooden cross with thin black cords.

I tie an ox's bladder in front of her belly.

I smear her whole body with two kilograms of lard.

I break a hen's egg over the ox's bladder.

I sprinkle her with sour milk.

I pour tomato sauce over her.

I dust her with flour.

I dip rags into paint and stuff them under the cords so that they hang down like guts out of her body.

I spray the body with soda-water.

I throw paint-powder over her body.

I obliterate the cross.

I release her arms from the cords and tear down the crosspiece which was fastened with pegs, and bind it between her legs so that she rides it like a witch.

I bind her more tightly to the wood with rags, cords and plastic tubing.

I lay the whole structure on the ground.

> I pour beer over it, spray it with soda-water and break twenty hens' eggs over it.
>
> I throw over it three kilograms of breadcrumbs, five kilograms of black powder-paint, five litres of sour milk, waste paper and rubbish, and pack it all into a large plastic bag.
>
> (MS. 1963)

This is a symbolic action with a universal meaning. It is more than the realisation of anal and anal-sadistic impulses, and its significance goes further than the fact that during the war Otto Mühl was deeply impressed by the 'horrible beauty' of the bodies of his comrades, smeared with blood and dirt, frozen to the ground and covered with hoar-frost.[31] The substances with which the 'crucified' model was pelted are symbols of the *prima materia* – the primeval stuff of the great Earth-Mother – which plays an important part in the gnostic and alchemistic tradition[32] (sludge, the black cloud, the gelatinous materials, and so on) and of the fertility aspects of this *prima materia* (the foodstuffs, particularly the eggs). In the first part the central Christ-figure, by being fettered and covered with primeval slime, is 'utterly obliterated'. In the second part the picture changes to that of a witch-like earth-mother who is finally – through the packing in a plastic bag – returned to an embryonic state. The extreme anti-spiritual trend and the relationship with elements of the Satan cult are obvious. A discussion of the production of such 'actions', appearing in the *Frankfurter Allgemeine Zeitung*, very reasonably says: 'Without question . . . they go back . . . to . . . atavistic impulses that linger in the secret places of the human soul and may be activated at any time. Only the most superficial observer will be surprised that it is once more in this town of wine and waltzes that they have found open expression.'[33]

Hermann Nitsch introduced the 'crucifixion and dismemberment of the lamb' into action theatre.[34] This 'primeval excess' is also the focal point of his action drama *König Ödipus* (MS. 1964). Nitsch gives his own interpretation in the manifesto *das lamm*:

> Starting from the sensible reality of the flayed corpse wet with blood, we can associate to the beginnings of the myth. The

group of assocations thus released is directly involved with the control of the collective upsurges of human vitality which constantly drive men to orgies. The lamb mainly appears in symbolic connection with these impulses and their terminal points, sublimations and repressions. The Dionysian surge of emotion ends in the dismemberment of the god Dionysus (the bull symbolising him), it ends in excess. The negative image of the Dionysian orgy, the Passion, ends in the masochistic excess of sacrifice. The informal, concrete breaking through of primitive impulses in art is exactly the same as the essence of the Dionysian cult, for its consequence is emotion taken to the extreme point of excess. O.M. Theater, or action theatre, makes use of this phenomenon, and achieves a regression within art, an emergence of the Dionysian element. The dismemberment of the lamb is a symbolic treatment, carried out in O.M. Theater, of the primeval experience of excess (the ecstatic terminal point of the orgy of abreaction). The real sadomasochistic situation of the dismemberment of the lamb, as it appears to the senses, is identical with an extreme outbreak of primitive impulses.[35]

Although we have not attempted a complete picture, we have tried in this chapter to present a mosaic of phenomena as diverse as possible, to show that the Satan cult and its fringe phenomena are active even in this century.

CONCLUSION

Basically there are three possible attitudes towards the tradition of Satan worship. We can, as happens most frequently, adopt the traditional Christian position, judge the Satan cult harshly and reject it. Or we can more or less identify ourselves with it. Or, finally, we can judge it from a distance, taking into account both its negative and destructive and its positive and creative aspects. We have tried to follow the last course in this study, and we hope to do the same in the following concluding remarks.

First we should say that the Christian world has never quite lost the sense of the complete entity, composed of darkness and light, of both God and man. There still exists a wide stream of tradition, mostly outside the accepted doctrine of the Church, to support this. This tradition culminates in alchemy, whose beginnings can be traced back to the third century AD,[1] and which had a second – though epigonal – flowering in the seventeenth century. The work of the alchemists, which, as modern depth psychology has shown, has exact parallels with psychic processes, was always directed at the unifying of opposites into one complete whole.[2] One of these symbols of wholeness is the *Deus terrestris* (earthly God) or *filius macrocosmi* (son of the macrocosm),[3] comparable with the Gnostic 'Anthropos' or primeval man.[4] Primeval man as the *anima mundi* or world-soul contains within himself the four elements, denoting completeness.

The doctrine of the Rosicrucians,[5] whose name has been derived from that of their legendary founder Christian Rosenkreutz (who is supposed to have died in 1484 at the age of 106, was also based on the idea of the union of opposites. Their symbol is the combination of the rose with the cross, that is to say nature with supernature.

It is impossible to give here even an outline of the tradition brought to mind by the mention of the alchemists and the Rosicrucians. It has numberless ramifications (including the different trends in Freemasonry). We should have to talk about the transmitters of this tradition – Joachim of Floris, Paracelsus, Jacob Boehme, and certain nature philosophers of the romantic period. The same stock of ideas has propagated itself down to our time; it survives to a considerable extent, in more or less corrupt

The *'filius macrocosmi'* of the Alchemists.

form, in the doctrine and rites of today's secret societies.[6] Its effective nucleus is the conception of a completeness overshadowing the Christian dualism of light and dark, celestial and earthly, spiritual and sensual, male and female, and so on.

But even in the Christian church itself a fragment of the light-and-dark wholeness of the divine and the human has survived. Apart from the fact that a few passages in the Bible and many liturgical words and actions are non-dualistic,[7] there are some interesting religious phenomena that fall outside the tradi-

The Rose Cross.

tional Apollonian background. Probably the most important example is a mystery cult in modern Greece:

> One of the less known curiosities of modern Greece is the religious cult of a small group of believers who practise, within the Orthodox faith, a special veneration of an archaic Dionysian type for Saints Constantine, Helena and Soteris. An unusual feature of their orgiastic festivals is that on certain feast-days the faithful appear to acquire the power of fire-walking. With their icons in their hands, they can walk barefoot over flaming coals at between 200° and 300°C, and emerge unhurt.
>
> They call themselves 'Anastenaria', meaning 'aspirants'. Their members are both male (Anastenaris) and female (Anas-

tenarissa or Anastenara). They also give the name 'Anastenaria' to the festivals held on the saints' name-days. Their leader is the Archianastenaris. The adherents of this sect are mainly simple peasants who can neither read nor write. They were discovered only recently by the president of the Society for Psychical Research in Athens, Professor Tanagras, who succeeded in obtaining a promise from both Church and State that they would not issue any ban against them on account of their pagan rites. This was the only possible way of gaining the confidence of these withdrawn and exclusive people and inducing them to show their strange religious practices openly.

The historical origin of this cult goes far back into the pre-Christian era, to the Phrygians, who also walked through fire. The Pontians, who lived on the shores of the Black Sea, took over this custom as part of their cult of Dionysus. Later the Byzantine emperors settled this warlike Greek race in northern and eastern Thrace as a protection against the Bulgars, and there, living on lonely heights, they could continue their cult unobserved; there too the wild Thracian cult had originated in very ancient times. After the cession of northern Thrace to Bulgaria in 1914, some of the Thracians, and with them some of the Anastenaria, fled to Macedonia and settled there. There is still a group of Anastenaria in Bulgaria today. They hold their festivals, as was customary with the old mysteries, secretly and at night. The faithful roll embers from the hearth over the earthen floor and dance in their closed festival hall, which they call Konaki. This cult-form is a combination of pagan elements with rites from the recognised State religion, which has also kept pagan features up to the present day.

Feast-days begin with a normal Orthodox service, followed by water consecration and an animal sacrifice, in the manner we know from the Eleusinian mysteries, the cult of St Kabir and the Orphic cult. Formerly the sacrificial animal was bought out of the common fund to which the faithful subscribe a fixed proportion of their income. As in ancient times, sacrificial pits are dug and the bones and internal organs put into them. The age of the sacrificial animal, an untamed bull or a ram, must be an odd number. The strongly rural nature of the proceedings is particularly noticeable in the fact that the sacrifice is coupled with a consecration of the fields. The Archianastenaris waves a sacred red cloth in benediction over the fields towards every point of the compass, and continues to dance until the animal is finally sacrificed.

All cult practices involve processions, in which the Anastenaria take their icons with them. These have been copied for eight hundred years from an original in Constantinople. Very special icons, handed down from generation to generation, with which their ancestors walked through fire, bear the name 'dancing icons'. They are surrounded by an ornate silver frame and decorated with the red cloths which are kept through the year in a little cabinet under the iconostasis. We meet this chest in the cult of Demeter, where it contained the most sacred garments which, like the red cloths here, threw mystics into ecstasy. In the afternoon of the first day the Anastenaria reach such a pitch of ecstasy that they experience the need to touch the purifying fire. For the newly initiated this is the moment when 'the saint lays hands on them' or 'the image of the pure one calls', as they say.

In the midst of the ecstasy very distinctive sounds can be perceived, partly like a dog barking, partly a long-drawn-out hiss. Particularly remarkable are the impulsively uttered cries of 'hach', 'ich', 'ech', which appear to be forms of Iakchus = Bacchus. Formerly the image of this god was carried in procession, as the icons are now, from Athens to Eleusis.

According to authorities on comparative religion, the theme of purification through fire, or of the union of the human with the divine, is expressed in these practices.

A special virtue attributed to the ancient mystics was silence. So whatever we cannot see with our eyes, feel with our emotions, or deduce from what we see or hear, we shall never know from the lips of the Anastenaria. As with the Eleusinian mysteries, so here too the last and deepest secret remains hidden.[8]

There are further examples to be found in the Ethiopian Church, in which the dance of the priests, accompanied by clapping, stamping and musical instruments, has survived to this day,[9] or the Gospel singing at Negro services in the Southern States of America.[10]

But to an even greater extent culture in general, including the arts, in every epoch, has developed tendencies opposed to Christian dualism. This was most overwhelmingly the case at the Renaissance and in the Romantic period. The depth psychology of the twentieth century and the last years of the nineteenth is of particular importance from this point of view. Freud was the first to break through the traditional Christian taboos, which rest on the same foundations as the Satan cult, and Jung, whose psychology is built round the conception of 'self' as a complete entity, reaches as the culminating point of his work the question of how it is possible 'to accept and endure, without perishing, the dark god who also wants to become man'.[11] Erich Neumann, in his book *Tiefenpsychologie und neue Ethik*, has laid the foundations for an ethical system that is no longer dualistic:

> Whereas the final conception of the old ethics was division, differentiation and fission, as formulated in the mythological projection of the Last Judgement as a separation of the sheep from the goats, the good from the evil, the guiding principle of the new ethics is the union of opposites in a homogeneous structure. . . . The aim . . . is to achieve completeness – the total personality. . . . All . . . power groups must be taken into account, since, as in the collective life of nations, repression or inhibition leads to reactions which could shake to its foundations the life of the community, and cause permanent unrest.[12]

The aim of freeing man from the necessity to choose between the two traditionally opposing principles and to enable him to see himself as a complete, universal being is also that of Existentialism. The contemporary artist who has shown us, without regression, a complete all-embracing totality is Picasso.

Let us try now to reach some definite conclusions.

The importance of the Satan cult does not lie primarily in the fact that phenomena of this kind still exist today, or that belief in witches is still fairly widespread in our time;[13] but that it reflects one of the most fundamental problems of Christian religion and culture as though in a concave mirror. Every member of a Christian civilisation shares in this problem even if he has turned away from Christianity, or actively opposes or rejects it. The effects of a process of fission that has gone on for almost two thousand years must reach down into deep layers of the psyche which are completely independent of the conscious mind.

It would be quite wrong to treat the dualistic tradition of Christianity as a simple misdevelopment. With all the negative aspects that go with it, it is a secular variant, that is both historically and psychologically inevitable. Today, however, when neurosis is attacking individuals and – in an applied sense – nations and ethnic groups to a menacing degree, the question of a synthesis[14] on a higher, that is to say not a pre-dualistic plane, becomes a very pressing one. It is necessary to retract the projections through which parts of one's own personality, other individuals or groups are brought under Satanic influence. But that will only happen when dualism is overcome at its very foundation – the relationship with the divine.

As far as we can see, it will be possible for comparatively few people to take this step, which, to be effective, must neither naively ignore the past nor wilfully anticipate the future. We cannot yet tell when – in the words of Kleist – 'the last chapter of history' will begin.

NOTES

PREFACE

1 Water Hollstein, 'Der Untergrund', *Soziologie jugendlicher Protestbewegungen*, Neuwied and Berlin, p. 7 (1969).
2 The ideas of Wilhelm Reich already played an important part in the Beat Generation [see *Beat: Eine Anthologie*, ed. by Karl O. Paetel, Rowohlt Paperback, Reinbeck bei Hamburg, *passim* (1962)]. In Germany the numerous pirated editions of Reich's writings make his influence obvious.
3 See Peter Priestley, 'Charles Manson und die Scientologen', in *Stuttgarter Zeitung*, (10 January 1970).
4 We can take as an example the sacrilege at Kleve in September 1968. See 'Unbekannter schmierte Satan-Sprüche in die Kirche. Gotteshaus auch mit Hakenkreuzen verunziert', *NRZ* (7 September 1968).
5 See the Carnival report 'Blösse im Bürgerbräu', *Stern*, No. 8, Hamburg (23 February 1969). In the St Pauli Nachrichten, Hamburg, the following advertisement appeared: 'Black Masses in all West German cities – Interested parties should contact Box 4300 Essen . . . ' (20 March 1970/No. 38).
6 On this phenomenon see Hans Mayer, 'Bildung, Besitz und Theater, Vortrag auf dem Volksbühnentag in Saarbrücken, 1968', extract in *Der Spiegel*, Hamburg (27 May 1968).
7 See Documents on the Satan cult and the Black Mass, Chapter 5, note 40, last item.
8 In *Psyche*, Stuttgart, year XXIII, No. 7, pp. 481ff (July 1969).
9 ibid., p. 147.
10 Philip Whalen, '4:2:59 Take I', in *Fuck you(!) Underground poems*, edited by Ralf-Rainer Rygulla, p. 22 (Darmstadt 1968).
11 On genital love in 'Die Urformen der Liebe und die Technik der Psychoanalyse', *Psychologisches Verständnis und medizinische Praxis*, 5, pp. 136ff, Berne and Stuttgart (1966).
12 ibid., p. 147.

INTRODUCTION

1 Vol. X, Rome 1953, col. 1953 (Antonio Romeo).
2 Satanic phenomena falling within the sphere of other religions are influenced by Christianity. Examples are the cult of the Moslem devil worshippers, and the Kurdish Yezidis (see Louis Massignon, 'Les Yezidis du Mont Sindjar *adorateurs d'Iblis*', in *Satan (Études Carmélitaines)*, pp. 175ff, Paris (1948).
3 Russell Hope Robbins, *The Encyclopedia of Witchcraft and Demonology*, p. 50, London (1960).

4 This term has become popular since the appearance of Erich Neumann's standard work, *Die Grosse Mutter: Der Archetyp des Grossen Weiblichen*, Zürich (1916).
5 See G. van der Leeuw, *Phänomenologie der Religion*, Tübingen, pp. 768ff (1956).
6 ibid., pp. 768f.
7 ibid., p. 787.
8 This idea originated with the philosophy of Edmund Husserl; it is used in a wider sense by religious phenomenology.
9 See C. G. Jung, 'Aion', *Psychol. Abhandlungen*, **VIII**, p. 391, Zürich (1951); and the same author's 'Psychologie und Alchemie', ibid., **V**, pp. 397f, Zürich (1952).

THE ORIGINS

1 *The Religious and Cultural Basis of Satan Worship*

1 'Die Herkunft der Dionysosreligion nach dem heutigen Stand der Forschung', Arbeit. Forsch. Landes *Nordrhein-Westf.*, *Geisteswiss.*, no. 58, Cologne and Opladen (1956).
2 See Karl Kerényi, *Die Mythologie der Griechen*, p. 261, Zürich (1951).
3 See Karl Kerényi, *Griechische Miniaturen*, p. 120, Zürich (1957).
4 *Theophania* (ŕowohlts deutsche enzyklopädie) **15** p. 117, Hamburg (1956). (Reproduced without italics.)
5 See Karl Kerényi, 'Das Problem des Bösen in der Mythologie, in *Das Böse* (Studien aus dem C. G. Jung-Institut Zürich, **XIII**), pp. 23f, Zürich and Stuttgart (1961).
6 Homeric Hymn to Pan. Translated from *Homerische Hymnen*, p. 119, ed. by Anton Weiher (Tusculum-Bücherei), Munich (1951).
7 Rudolf Bultmann, *Das Urchristentum* (rowohlts deutsche enzyklopädie) 157/158, p. 146, Hamburg (1962). See also Eduard Stemplinger, *Antiker Volksglaube (Sammlung Volksglaube), Stuttgart (* 1948); Georg Luck, *Hexen und Zauberei in der römischen Dichtung (Sammlung Lebendige Antike)*, Zürich (1962)
8 Concerning *Saturnalia*, see Hedwig Kenner, *Das Phänomen der Verkehrten Welt in der griechisch-romischen Antike* (Ans Forschung und Kunst, vol. 8), Klagenfurth (1970).
9 Yasna 45, 2.
10 Bultmann, op. cit., p. 152f.
11 In C. G. Jung, 'Symbolik des Geistes', *Psychol. Abhandlungen*, **VI,** Zürich (1955). All references are given there.
12 Schärf, op. cit., p. 317.
13 See Victor Maag, 'Der Antichrist als Symbol des Bosen', in *Das Böse*, pp. 63–89.
14 See Franz Cumont, *Die Mysterien des Mithra*, Darmstadt (1963).
15 See Bultmann, op. cit., p. 153.
16 Chap. XII, Migne PG VIII, 240f.
17 Migne PG XXXIII, 1068ff.

18 See the detailed bibliography in *Satan* (Études Carmélitaines), pp. 647ff.
19 In Joanem XXVII, 10. Migne PL XXXV, 1620.

2 *Sociological Aspects of Satanic Movements*

1 In *Uppsala Universitets-Arskrift (Acta Universitatis Upsaliensis) 1951*, No. 5, Uppsala-Wiesbaden (1951). See especially pp. 308ff.
2 See Levis A. Coser, *The function of social conflict*, Glencoe, Ill. (1956).
3 An analysis from the point of view of group sociology – relating, however, only to the inquisitors – of a historic witch trial is to be found in Wanda von Baeyer, 'Die historischen Hexenprozesse', in *Massen wahn in Geschichte und Gegenwart*, ed. by Wilhelm Bitter, Stuttgart 1965.
4 Piper Paperback, p. 488 Munich (1963).

3 *The Psychopathological Features of Satan Worship*

1 Definition by J. L. A. Koch in his work *Die psychopathischen Minderwertigkeiten*, 3 volumes, Ravensburg (1891–3).
2 *Collected Works*, Vol. XIII, pp. 315–53, London (1955). See also Rudolf Löwenstein, 'Zur Psychoanalyse der Schwarzen, Messen', in *Imago*, Vienna, (1923) IX (1), pp. 73ff (1923); Henry Lowenfeld, 'Über den Niedergang des Teufelsglaubens und seine Folgen für die Massenpsychologie', in *Psyche*, Stuttgart, **XXI** (7), July 1967 pp. 513ff (July 1967).
3 Note by Freud: see Th. Reik, *Der eigene und der fremde Gott*, Imago-Bücher III (1923), chapter: Gott and Teufel.
4 Freud, op. cit., p. 531f.
5 ibid., p. 333.
6 See Anna Freud, *Das Ich und die Abwehrmechanismen* (Kindler Taschenbücher 2001) Munich (1964).
7 Formulated according to Rudolf Brun, *Allgemeine Neurosenlehre*, p. 239, Basel (1954).

DOCUMENTS RELATING TO THE SATAN CULT AND THE BLACK MASS

4 *Fringe Manifestations of the Satan Cult in the First Centuries of the Christian Era*

1 *Die Gnosis* (Kröners Taschenausgabe, Volume 32), p. 186, Stuttgart (1955).
2 See Leonhard Fendt, *Gnostische Mysterien*, p. 9, Munich (1922).
3 More detailed information in Fendt, op. cit., pp. 12ff.
5 On mana see van der Leeuw, op. cit., pp. 4ff. On sperm and mana see Will-Erich Peuckert, *Geheimkulte*, pp. 396ff Heidelberg (1951).
6 See Stemplinger, op. cit., p. 104.
7 Supporting evidence in Hans Leisegang, *Pneuma Hagion* (published by the Forschunginstitut f. vergl. Rel. geschichte, University of Leipzig, No. 4), pp. 71f, Leipzig (1922).

8 Leisegang, Die Gnosis, p. 195.
9 See the relevant passages in the histories of dogma (Loofs, Harnack, Seeberg, etc.). The Logos-epicleses of many old liturgies belong in this context.
10 See Hans Lietzmann, *Messe und Herrenmahl* (Arbeiten z. Kirchengesch., 8), Bonn (1926).
11 See Thomas Ohm, *Die Gebetsgebärden der Völker und das Christentum*, pp. 438ff, Leiden (1948).
12 For the interpretation see Fendt, op. cit., pp. 20ff. Fendt's view is one-sided insofar as the establishing words actually belong in the context of the Eucharist (see Leitzmann, op. cit., *passim*).
13 Fendt, op. cit., p. 20.
14 See Heinrich Ploss and Max Bartels, *Das Weib in der Natur- und Völkerkunde*, Vol. 1, pp. 519ff, Leipzig (1913). Julius Evola, *Metaphysik des Sexus*, pp. 246ff, Stuttgart (1962); Stemplinger, op. cit., p. 105.
15 Quoted in Ploss-Bartels, op. cit., p. 521.
16 Neumann, *Die Grosse Mutter*, p. 149.
17 See ibid., pp. 149ff.
18 See Leisegang, *Die Gnosis*, pp. 111ff.
19 The name is derived from the Greek 'peraō – pass beyond. The meaning is 'going beyond the transient'.
20 From the many writing on snake-symbolism we may mention: Jacob Maehly, *Die Schlange im Mythus und Cultus der classischen Völker*, Leipzig (1867); Erich Küster, 'Die Schlange in der griechischen Kunst und Religion', in *Religionsgesch. Versuche u. Verarb.*, **XIII** (2), Giessen (1913); Albrecht Dieterich, 'Abraxas' in *Festschrift für H. Usener*, Leipzig (1891); Hans Leisegang, 'Das Mysterium der Schlange', in *Eranos-Jahrbuch VII (1939)*, Zürich (1940); Article 'Schlange' in *Handwörterbuch des deutschen Aberglaubens*, Vol. VII, cols 1114ff, Berlin and Leipzig (1935); C. G. Jung, *Symbole der Wandlung*, *passim*, Zürich (1952). (See index.)

21 See Erich Neumann, *Ursprungsgeschichte des Bewusstseins*, pp. 53ff, Zürich (1949).
22 Eusebius Caes., *Praep. Evang.* I,10. Migne PG XXI, pp. 89f.
23 'Das Mysterium der Schlange', in op. cit., pp. 150–252.
24 Hippolyt. Elench. V.
25 See the text in Leisegang, *Die Gnosis*, p. 145.
26 See Franz Diekamp, *Katholische Dogmatik*, Vol. 3, pp. 130ff, Münster i. Westf. (1942).
27 Fendt, op. cit., p. 24.
28 PG CXXII, 817–76.
29 See the summary of findings in Carl Andresen, 'Die Kritik der Alten Kirche am Tanz der Spätantike', in *Der Tanz in der modernen Gesellschaft*, pp. 139ff, ed. Friedrich Heyer, Hamburg (1958). This also contains a large number of sources for the phenomenon.
30 Migne PG LVIII, 491.
31 Further detail in the author's *Psyche und Mysterium* (Studien aus dem C. G. Jung-Institut Zürich, V), pp. 57ff, 152ff, Zürich (1954).

5 *The Medieval Golden Age of Satan Worship*

1 See E. Louis Backmann, *Religious Dances in the Christian Church and in Popular Medicine*, pp. 170ff, London (1952); Curt Sachs, *Eine Weltgeschichte des Tanzes*, pp. 170ff, Berlin (1953); Ernesto de Martino, *La Terra del Bimorso, Contributo una Storia Religiosa del Sud*, Milan (1961).
2 See Backmann, op, cit., pp. 172ff.
3 As early as 879, the temple of Swantewit on Arkona was turned into a chapel of St Vitus, to which sufferers from dance-mania were brought to be cured. See Max von Boehn, *Der Tanz* (7th annual series of the Volksverb. d. Bücherfreunde, Vol. 2) p. 65, Berlin (1925).
4 See Giraldus Cambrensis, *Itinerarium Cambriae* I, 2. Text given in Sachs, op. cit., p. 171.
5 Collected works, Musarion edition, Vol. III, Munich 1920, p. 25.
6 See Du Cange, *Glossarium mediae et infimae Latinitatis*, nova editio, Vol. IV, pp. 277f, Paris (1938) (under 'Cervula'). There is an interpretation in Paul Radin, Karl Kerényi, C. G. Jung, *Der göttliche Schelm*, pp. 187ff, Zürich (1954).
7 The custom of choosing a child bishop has survived to this day in many places, such as the monastery of Montserrat.
8 See Backmann, op. cit., p. 193 (caption to illustration).
9 See Du Cange, op. cit., Vol. VI, pp. 253f Paris (1938) (under 'Pelota'); Hugo Rahner, *Der spielende Mensch*, p. 74, Einsiedeln (1952) Alfons Rosenberg, *Die christliche Bildmeditation*, pp. 278ff, München-Planegg (1955); Siegfried Mendner, *Das Ballspiel im Leben der Völker*, pp. 69f, Münster i. Westf. (1956).
10 See Du Cange, op. cit., Vol. III, pp. 460f, Paris (1938), (under 'Festum Asinorum'). There is an explanation in Radin, Kerényi, Jung, op. cit. pp. 188ff.
11 For the symbolism of the ass see J. Collin de Plancy, *Dictionnaire infernal*, nouv. éd., pp. 32f, Paris (1853); Forstner, op. cit. pp. 367ff.
12 Walter F. Otto, *Dionysos* (Frankf. Studien z. Religion u. Kultur d. Antike, Volume IV), p. 155, Frankfurt a.M. (1960).
13 In the fourth part.
14 On the history of medieval heretical movements see Arno Borst, *Die Katharer* (Schriften d. Monumenta Germaniae historica, 12), Stuttgart (1953). This also gives comprehensive references.
15 For essential information on sources I am indebted to Prof. Arno Borst and Prof. Hans Martin Klinkenberg (see Preface).
16 On the survival of Manicheism in the Middle Ages see Steven Runciman, *The Medieval Manichee*, Cambridge (1947).
17 See Borst, op. cit., pp. 151ff.
18 See Caufeynon and Jaf, *Les Messes Noires*, pp. 28ff, Paris (1905).
19 See Borst, op. cit., pp. 74f.
20 See Evola, op. cit., pp. 173ff.
21 ibid., p. 175.
22 See Stemplinger, op. cit., p. 115.
23 See Borst, op. cit., pp. 75f.

24 See Forstner, op. cit., pp. 376f.
25 For example Eucherius of Lyons, *Liber formul.*, V, Migne PG I, 753 (mentioned by Forstner, p. 376).
26 See Ohm, op. cit., pp. 224f.
27 See Collin de Plancy, op. cit., pp. 135f.
28 See the corresponding key-words (Socialism, etc.) in the index to Borst, op. cit.
29 On the ritual of the witches' sabbath we mention only the following works: Jules Baissac, *Les grands jours de la Sorcellerie*, pp. 94ff, Paris (1890); Caufeynon and Jaf, *Les Messes Noires*, pp. 153ff) Jules Bois, *Le Satanisme et la Magie*, pp. 93ff, Paris (1896); Jules Michelet, *La Sorcière* (Société des textes franc. mod.), new critical edition, Vol. I, pp. 127ff, Paris (1952).
30 op. cit., p. 430.
31 op. cit., p. 127.
32 See Kurt Buschwitz, *Hexen und Hexenprozesse*, pp. 216ff, Munich (1963).
33 See Heinrich Marzell, *Zauberpflanzen Hexentränke* (Kosmos-Bibl., Vol. 241), pp. 45ff, Stuttgart 1963.
34 See Erich Haisch, *Der Hexenwahn*, *Ciba-Zeitschrift*, **9** (101) pp. 3367f and Bibliography p. 3380, Wehr/Baden (1963).
35 Hexensalben (witches' ointment) in *Medizinischer Monatsspiegel (Merck)*, No. 9, p. 169, Darmstadt (1960). cf. the report in *Der Stern*, Hamburg, of 2 April 1960 (XIII/No. 14). See esp. Hanscarl Leuner, 'Die toxische Ekstase', in *Beiträge zur Ekstase*, pp. 734, ed. Th. Spoerri, Basle-New York (1968).
36 See *Die Grosse Mutter*, p. 278.
37 See, among others, Gisbert Kranz, *Farbiger Abglanz*, p. 67, Nuremberg (1957).
38 Reinhard Herbig, *Pan*, pp. 17f, 33, Frankfurt a.M., (1949).
39 Eleventh Orphic Hymn to Pan. See Herbig, op. cit., pp. 68f.
40 See ibid., pp. 27ff.
41 See Otto, op. cit., pp. 71f.
42 See Herbig, op. cit., pp. 71f.
43 See Forstner, op. cit., pp. 396f.
44 See ibid., pp. 434ff.
45 Further detail ibid., pp. 381f.
46 We can connect with the phenomenon under discussion the view of medieval moral theologians that melancholy, in the existentialist sense, is diabolical in origin. Conscious clinging to melancholy, expressed by the Graeco-Latin word *acedia* (wrongly translated as 'sloth') became one of the seven deadly sins.
47 Conc. Trident. Sess. 7 can. 9.
48 See Heinrich Schurtz, *Altersklassen und Männerbünde*, Berlin (1902); Adolf Ellegard Jensen, *Beschneidung und Reifezeremonien bei Naturvölkern* (Studien z. Kulturkunde, Vol. I), Stuttgart (1933).
49 Compare the placing of the good and the evil at the Last Judgement (Matth. 25: 33).
50 See Lietzmann, op. cit. p. 175.
51 See ibid., p. 82.

52 See ibid., p. 186.
53 See Baschwitz, op. cit., pp. 212ff.
54 *Die Grosse Mutter*, pp. 147ff.
55 It is significant that the dogma of Mary as the Mother of God was proclaimed (431) in Ephesus, the city of the many-breasted Diana. Unlike Western Christianity, Eastern Christianity has kept the early image of Mary in its essentials to this day.
56 See Marie-Madeleine Davy, 'Das Symbol der kosmischen Mutter im 12 Jahrhundert', in *Antaios*, **II** (2), pp. 158ff, Stuttgart (1960).
57 See Anne Marie Heiler, 'Die Stellung der Frau in den Religionen', in *Krisis und Zukunft der Frau*, pp. 158ff, ed Wilhelm Bitter, Stuttgart (1962).
58 See ibid., p. 203.
59 *Hist. Forschungen u. Quellen*, **12**, Munich and Freising (1936).
60 ibid., p. 62.
61 Geheimkulte, op. cit., pp. 267ff.
62 See under 'Blocksberg' in *Handwörterbuch des deutschen Aberglaubens*, Vol. I, cols 1423ff (1927); Will-Erich Peuckert, Der Blocksberg, in the same author's *Verborgenes Niedersachsen*, pp. 103ff, Göttingen (1960).
63 On the importance of Diana (mentioned in the Canon Episcopi around 900) for medieval witchcraft, see Anton Mayer, op. cit., p. 18; Henry Charles Lea, *Geschichte der Inquisition im Mittelalter*, Vol. 3, p. 552, Bonn (1913).
64 op. cit., Vol. 1, pp. 135ff.
65 Joseph Hansen, *Quellen und Untersuchungen zur Geschichte des Hexenwahns und der Hexenverfolgung im Mittelalter*, p. 38, Bonn (1901).
66 In *Antaios*, **I**(1), p. 1ff Stuttgart (1959).
67 See Fritz Weege, *Der Tanz in der Antike*, p. 69, Halle/Saale (1926).
68 See Anton Mayer, op. cit., pp. 49ff.
69 On the sexual symbolism of trees see Jean Boullet, *Symbolisme sexuel* (Bibl. intern d'érotologie), pp. 13f, Paris (1961); Lo Duca, *L'Érotisme au Cinéma III* (Bibl. intern. d'érotologie), pp. 54ff, Paris (1962).
70 See Neumann, *Die Grosse Mutter*, p. 68f, 278.
71 ibid., pp. 148, 166, 183f.
72 See Otto, op. cit., pp. 94ff.; Kerényi, *Die Mythologie der Griechen*, pp. 252ff.
73 725ff. Translation by Arthur S. Way, *Euripides in English Verse*, Volume III, p. 402, London (1898).
74 See, among others, Karl Kerényi, *Streifzüge eines Hellenisten*, p. 55ff, Zürich (1960).
75 See Karl Simrock, *Handbuch der Deutschen Mythologie mit Einschluss der nordischen*, p. 216ff, Bonn (1864).
76 See ibid., pp. 375ff.
77 Edda, Havamal, 139.
78 Neumann, *Die Grosse Mutter*, p. 264.
79 On the mother-symbolism of the Cross see Jung, *Symbole der Wandlung*, pp. 463ff.
80 See Simrock, op. cit., pp. 236f.
81 See for example Heribert Jone, *Katholische Moraltheologie*, Innsbruck (1961).

82 See Neumann, *Die Grosse Mutter*, pp. 101f.
83 Vol. 4, part 2, p. 263, Regensburg (1842).
84 See Sigmund Freud, 'Drei Abhandlungen zur Sexualtheorie', in Coll. works, Vol. V, pp. 27–145 (1949).
85 See Wilhelm Reich, *Der Einbruch der Sexualmoral*, Copenhagen (1935); Bronislaw Malinowski, *Geschlecht und Verdrängung in primitiven Gesellschaften* (rowohlts deutsche enzyklopädie, 139/140), Reinbek bei Hamburg (1962); op. cit., bibliography pp. 274ff.
86 See Jung, *Symbole der Wandlung, passim*; Neumann, *Ursprungsgeschichte des Bewusstseins, passim.*
87 See C. G. Jung, 'Von den Wurzeln des Bewusstseins', in *Psychol. Abhandlungen*, **IX** pp. 84f, Zürich (1954).
88 op. cit., p. 208.
89 See Groddeck, *Das Buch vom Es, Psychoanalytische Shriften zur Literatur und Kunst*, esp. pp. 9ff, 268ff, Wiesbaden (1964).
90 ibid., p. 269.
91 See the author's 'Sexus und Individuation', *Praxis der Psychotherapie*, **VIII** (6), pp. 268ff, Munich (1963).
92 On the succubus see Robbins, op. cit., pp. 234ff. cf. the same author's comments on the incubus, pp. 490ff.
93 For example, that of D. H. Lawrence and Henry Miller.
94 op. cit., pp. 137f.
95 op. cit., Vol. 1, p. 139, note.
96 *La Messe Noire*, p. 62, Paris (1958).
97 See Edwin Oliver James, *Religionen der Vorzeit* (DuMont Dokumente), p. 145, Cologne (1960); Sachs, op. cit., pp. 46f.
98 Sachs, op. cit., p. 258. On the Branle see also loc. cit., ff; Fritz Felmann, 'Historische Tänze der musikalischen und choreo-graphischen Weldliteratur', Part I, in *Volkstanz im Tanzarchiv*, 4 Jahrg., 5. Heft, pp. 73ff Hamburg (1960).
99 See Sachs, op. cit., pp. 295f.
100 See Forstner, op. cit., pp. 337ff.
101 op. cit., pp. 42ff.
102 See Kranz, op. cit., pp. 74.
103 Also spelt Rays, Raiz, Retz. On Gilles de Rais see Lea, op. cit., Vol. 3, pp. 529ff; Roland Villeneuve, *Gilles de Rays* (Coll. La Tour Saint-Jacques), Paris (1955) (with detailed list of sources and bibliography); Georg Bataille, *Gilles de Rais*, Hamburg (1968).
104 Confession de Gilles, 22 October 1440. Quoted in Villeneuve, op. cit., p. 174, note.
105 Déposition de Poitou, 17 October 1440. Also quoted by Villeneuve.
106 First edition Paris 1840. On this book see Chapter 7, c, of the present work.
107 *Là-bas*, pp. 51f, 53, Paris (1891).
108 Among the abundant literature on the subject we may mention: Lea, op. cit., Vol. 3, pp. 269ff.; Konrad Schottmüller, *Der Untergang des Templerordens*, 2 vols, Berlin (1887); Heinrich Finke, *Papsttum und Untergang des Templerordens*, 2 vols. (Vorreformationsgeschichtl. Forschungen, 4 & 5)

Münster i. Westf. (1907); Raymond Oursel, *Le Procés des Templiers*, Paris (1955).

109 *Geheimlehre und Geheimstatuten des Tempelherrenordens*, Berlin (1879); ibid., *Entwicklung und Untergang des Tempelherrenordens*, Berlin (1888).

110 op. cit., Vol 3, p. 301.

111 See ibid., pp. 313f.

112 *Édition Michelet*, Vol. II, p. 195.

113 See Ohm, op. cit., pp. 184f. The taboo placed on the navel by film censorship in the USA is of interest in this context.

114 Trial of Gérard du Passage on 27 April 1310. Michelet, Vol. I, p. 212.

115 See Collin de Plancy, op. cit., p. 468. A study on Baphomet, the interpretation of which is, however, not reliably supported, can be found in Roland Villeneuve, *Le Diable*, (Bibl. intern. d'érotologie), p. 57, Paris (1963).

116 See Lea, op. cit., Vol. 3, pp. 503f. A very exaggerated and far-fetched, but interesting, explanation can be found in Julius Evola, *Das Mysterium des Grals, pp.* 179ff, München-Planegg (1955).

6 *The Private Character of the Black Mass at the Time of Louis XIV*

1 See Baschwitz, op. cit., pp. 222ff.

2 See the heading of the source document.

3 See G. Legué, *Médecins et Empoisonneurs au XVIIe siècle*, Paris (1896); Frantz Funck-Brentano, *Die Giftmord-Tragödie nach den Archiven der Bastille*, Munich (1903); Georges Mongredien, *Madame de Montespan et l'affaire des poisons*, Paris (1953) (with detailed bibliography and information on sources).

4 According to tradition Louise de Lavallière was the first to call him this.

5 Taken from *Toute la Danse*, Paris, Year 4, p. 28 (January 1955).

6 The words quoted are from the Ambrosian hymn *Splendor paternae gloriae* (Breviarum Romanum, Feria II ad Laudes). On Christian sun-symbolism see Franz Joseph Dölger, *Die Sonne der Gerechtigkeit und der Schwarze* (Liturgiegesch. Forschungen, Heft 2), Münster i. Westf. (1919); idem., *Sol Salutis*, Münster i. Westf. (1925); Forstner, op. cit., pp. 119ff.

7 See van der Leeuw, op. cit., pp. 450ff.; Neumann, *Die Grosse Mutter*, p. 270.

8 See Forstner, op. cit., pp. 520ff.

9 ibid., pp. 522ff.

10 See Stemplinger, op. cit., p. 128.

11 See the detailed passages in Ploss-Bartels, op. cit., Vol. 1, Leipzig (1913).

12 Combination of circular and quadrilateral constructions. On mandala symbolism see Jung, *Psychologie und Alchemie*, pp. 159ff.

13 Interrogatoire de Vautier du 2 novembre 1679 (Bibliothèque du Corps Législatif) Ravaisson VI, p. 37.

14 See Hermann L. Strack, *Das Blut im Glauben und Aberglauben der Menschheit*, Munich (1900); Theodor Schiffner, *Blutzauber und Anderes*, Leipzig (1930); Franz Rüsche, *Blut, Leben und Seele* (Studien z. Gesch. u. Kultur des Altertums, 5. Erg.bd) Paderborn (1930); Ornella Volta, *Le Vampire* (Bibl. intern. d'érotologie) Paris (1962).

15 *Völkerpsychologie*, Vol. II, part 2, p. 15, Leipzig (1906).
16 See F. M. Th. Böhl, 'Zum babylonische Ursprung des Labyrinths', in *Miscellanea Orientalia A. Deimel dedicata*, p. 21, Rome (1935); Karl Kerényi, *Labyrinth-Studien* (Series 'Albae Vigiliae', new series no. X), pp. 14f, Zürich (1950).
17 op. cit. Vol. VI, p. 336, note.
18 See Baschwitz, op. cit., pp. 238f.

7 *The Romantic Style of the Satan Cult in the Nineteenth Century*

1 Florence 1948. On the poetisation of the Satan-cult see also *Schwarze Messen–Dichtungen und Dokumente* (Bibliotheca Dracula Hanser), ed. Ulrich K. Dreikandt, Munich (1970).
2 See Charles Baudelaire, *Les Fleurs du Mal*, commentary pp. 419, 423 ed. Antoine Adam (Classiques Garnier), Paris (1961). Reference here to Louis Maigron, *Le Romantisme et les moeurs*, pp. 187f, Paris (1910).
3 Notes written 16 June 1860.
4 Mon coeur mis à nu.
5 1947. New edition (Coll. Idées), Paris (1963).
6 Sartre, op. cit., p. 88.
7 ibid., p. 239.
8 In Baudelaire, op. cit., p. 424.
9 On Leopardi see for example Karl Vossler, *Leopardi*, Heidelberg (1930); Francesco de Sanctis, *Studi sul Leopardi*, Naples (1955); G. Laini, *Leopardi*, Florence (1948).
10 See Friedrich Heiler, *Das Geber*, pp. 182ff, Munich (1921).
11 Diels, Fragm. 52.
12 On Carducci see among others A. Galletti, *L'opera di Giosuè Carducci*, Bologna (1929); W. F. Smith, *A bibliography of critical material on Giosuè Carducci*, Colorado Springs (1942).
13 On Huysmans see for example Jean Bricaud, *Huysmans et le Satanisme*, Paris (1913); Léon Deffoux, *J. K. Huysmans sous divers aspects*, Paris and Brussels (1943); Maurice Garçon, *Huysmans inconnu*, Paris (1941); Robert Baldick, *The life of J.-K. Huysmans*, Oxford (1955); Praz, op. cit., *passim*. For our introductory remarks we have made particular use of Jean Bricaud, 'Joris-Karl Huysmans als Okkultist und Magier', in *Hain der Isis*, Nos 4, 5 and 6, Brandenburg (1951).
14 Quoted according to Bricaud, in *Hain der Isis*, No. 4, p. 139.
15 See Kerényi, *Die Mythologie der Griechen*, pp. 173f.
16 See Hans Herter, *Vom dionysischen Tanz Zum komischen Spiel* (Darstellung und Deutung, no. 1) *passim*, Iserlohn (1947).
17 *Certains* (G. Moreau, Degas, Cheret, Whistler, Rops, Le Monstre, Le Fer), p. 78, Paris (1889).
18 Translation by Constance Garnett, pp. 267, 272, London (1912).
19 See Brun, op. cit., pp. 366f.
20 *Là-bas.*

8 *Epigonal Phenomena and Surrealist 'Alienation' of the Satan Cult in the Twentieth Century*

1 pp. 100ff, Zürich–Leipzig–Vienna (1926).
2 ibid., pp. 113f.
3 See René Fülöp-Miller, *Der heilige Teufel* (special edition), pp. 19ff, Berlin–Vienna–Leipzig (1927).
4 idem, *Geist und Gesicht des Bolschewismus*, p. 114.
5 ibid., p. 255.
6 See Friedrich Heiler, *Urkirche und Ostkirche* (Die katholische Kirche des Ostens und Westens, Vol. I), pp. 291ff, Munich (1937).
7 See for example Alfred Weber, op. cit., pp. 465f.
8 See Wilhelm Treue, 'Idee und Verwirklichung des Marxismus', in *Massenwahn in Geschichte und Gegenwart* (in preparation).
9 *Intern. Psychoan. Bibliothek*, No. 9, p. 116, Leipzig, Vienna and Zürich (1920).
10 See for example Christina Hole, *Mirror of Witchcraft*, London (1957); Ronald Holmes, *Witchcraft in British History*, London (1974).
11 On Crowley see esp. Aleister Crowley, *The Spirit of Solitude: An Autobiography*, 2 vols, London (1929); John Symonds, *The Great Beast*, London (1955); Pierre Victor, 'Aleister Crowley et sa magie', in *La Tour Saint-Jacques, Paris*, No. 10–12, pp. 105–123 (1957).
12 For reasons of copyright it is unfortunately not possible to give a textual example.
13 *Volksrecht*, Zürich (8 January 1953).
14 *Der Abend*, Berlin (7 May 1963). See also Harry Price, 'I know that Black Masses are being celebrated today' (interview), in *Nash's Pall Mall Magazine*, pp. 92f, February 1931.
15 *Life*, **36**(9) (18 May 1964).
16 *Quick*, Munich (29 October 1955).
17 On the Satan cult in present-day France, see Francis Barney, *Prière à Satan – Messes noires d'hier et d'aujourd'hui.* Paris (1957).
18 In his book *Dogme et rituel de la haute magie*, Paris (1861). The picture is reproduced in Robbins, op. cit. p. 133.
19 See Kurt Seligmann, *Das Weltreich der Magie*, pp. 336ff, Stuttgart (1958).
20 *Geschichte des Surrealismus*, p. 223, Cologne (1961).
21 *Petrusblatt*, Berlin (18 August 1946).
22 See Hans Habe, 'Der Teufel kam nach Rom', in *Revue*, Munich, No. 6 (10 February 1963). On the ban, see among others a report in the *Stadt-Anzeiger*, Cologne (12 February 1963).
23 See Luis Buñuel, *Viridiana* (Cinemathek. 4), Hamburg (1962). The premiere of the film took place in Cannes in May 1961. In the German version of the film, the 'photographing' sequence was cut out, and the cock crowed only once.
24 ibid., p. 75.
25 ibid, p. 8.
26 Epilogue by Theodor Kotulla, ibid., p. 95.
27 See Arthur Ramos, *O Folclore Negro do Brasil*, Rio de Janeiro (1954); José

Medeiros, *Candomblé*, Rio de Janeiro (1957); Roger Bastide, *Sociologia do Folclore Brasileiro*, São Paulo (1959).

28 From 'Derzeitige archaisch-ekstatische Massenbewegungen in Brasilien', in *Massenwahn in Geschichte und Gegenwart*.

29 Georg Heidingsfelder, 'Sektierer des Satans', in *Mann in der Zeit* (October 1950).

30 cf. the prayer '*Perceptio corporis tui*' in the Roman mass.

31 See Hilde Spiel, *Aus der Tiefe der Zeit*, in *Frankfurter Allgemeine Zeitung* (30 April 1964).

32 See Jung, *Mysterium Coniunctionis, passim*. (See references in index, pp. 398f under '*prima materia*'.)

33 Spiel, op. cit. On Otto Muehl see also: Otto Muehl, *Papa Omo*, Vienna (1967); idem, *Mama & Papa, Materialaktion* 63–69, Frankfurt a.M. (1969); Jutta Burghardt and Wilfried Reichart, '56 Aktionen zur Befreiung', in *Filmkritik*, Frankfurt a.M., Year 13, No. 10, pp. 611ff (October 1969); Peter Gorsen, *Das Bild Pygmalions – Kunstsoziologische Essays*, Rowohlt Paperback, Reinbek bei Hamburg (1969); idem, *Das Prinzip Obszön, rororo sexologie*, Reinbek bei Hamburg (1969); O. Tannebaum, *Dokumentation über Otto Muehls Materialaktion in der SHFBK Braunschweig und deren Folgen*, 2 parts, pub. by the Staatl. Hochschule für Bildende Künste in Brunswick (1970); the author's 'Abyssus abyssum invocat', in *Documents*, Strasbourg, year 25, pp. 78ff (May–June 1970).

34 See Prospectus of the Galerie Junge Generation, Vienna, No. 10 (Nitsch 24 June–4 July 1964;; Hermann Nitsch, *Orgien Mysterien Theater*, Darmstadt (1969); idem, *König Ödipus – Eine spielbare Theorie des Dramas*, Darmstadt (1972). See also Wilhelm Höck, 'Schmutz der sauberen Leute', in *Die Zeit*, Hamburg (1 May 1970); P. Willehad Paul Eckert, 'Zu den Materialaktionen von Otto Muehl und Hermann Nitsch', in *Das Böse, Dokumente und Interpretationen* (Series Hanser 89), pp. 41ff, ed. by the author, Munich (1972).

35 Published by the above-named Gallery.

CONCLUSION

1 See Marie Louise von Franz, 'Die alchemistische Makrokosmos–Mikrokosmos–Idee im Lichte der Jungschen Psychologie', in *Symbolon. Jahrbuch für Symbolforschung*, 1, pp. 27ff, Basle–Stuttgart (1960).

2 See Herbert Silberer, *Probleme der Mystik und ihrer Symbolik*, Vienna and Leipzig (1914) (published in a photostat edition in Darmstadt 1965); Jung, *Psychologie und Alchemie*, pp. 78ff, idem, *Mysterium Coniunctionis*.

3 See Jung, *Psychologie und Alchemie*, pp. 322f.

4 See C. G. Jung, *Paracelsica*, pp. 78ff, Zürich and Leipzig (1942).

5 Works on the Rosicrucians include: Gustav Krüger, *Die Rosenkreutzer*, Berlin (1932); Will-Erich Peuckert, *Die Rosenkreutzer*, Jena (1928); idem, *Pansophie*, pp. 369ff and *passim* (Berlin 1956).

6 See, for example, Pierre Geyraud, *Sectes et Rites – Petites Églises*, Religions nouvelles, *Sociétés Secrètes de Paris*, Paris (1954).

7 See the author's *Psyche und Mysterium, passim*.
8 Aranca, *Die Glut der Gläubigen*. Reprint from the *Stuttgarter Zeitung* (26 August 1960).
9 See Heiler, *Urkirche und Ostkirche*, p. 501.
10 See Joachim Ernst Berendt, *Das neue Jazzbuch* p. 98, Fischer Bücherei 270, Frankfurt a.M. (1959).
11 Antwort auf Hiob (1952) in Collected Works, Vol. 11, p. 491, Zürich and Stuttgart (1963).
12 (Kindler Taschenbücher, 2005), pp. 99f, Munich (1964).
13 See Herbert Auhofer, *Aberglaube und Hexenwahn heute*, Freiburg–Basle–Vienna (1960).
14 See, for example, Rosette Dubal, *La Psychanalyse du Diable* (Coll. 'Le chemin de la vie'), pp. 208ff, Paris (1953).

ORIGINAL LANGUAGE VERSIONS OF SOURCE DOCUMENTS

The following abbreviations appear in the information relating to the source documents.

Adam	Charles Baudelaire, *Les Fleurs du Mal.* Introduction, Relevé de Variantes et Notes par Antoine Adam (Classiques Garnier), Paris 1961.
Bouquet	M. Bouquet and others, *Recueil des historiens des Gaules et de la France*, Paris 1738–1904.
Carducci, Opere	*Edizione nazionale delle opere di Giosuè Carducci*, Bologna (1939 ff).
Du Cange	Du Cange, *Glossarium mediae et infimae Latinitatis*, nova editio, Paris (1938).
Fülöp-Miller	René Fülöp-Miller, *Geist und Gesicht des Bolschewismus*, Zürich–Leipzig–Vienna (1926).
Holl	Karl Holl, 'Epiphanius', in *Die griechischen christlichen Schriftsteller*, Vol. 25 (Vol. 1) and Vol. 31 (= Vol. 2) Leipzig (1915 and 1922).
Leisegang	Hans Leisegang, *Die Gnosis* (Kröners Taschenausgabe, Vol. 32), Stuttgart (1955).
Leopardi, Opere	Giacomo Leopardi, *Tutte le Opere* (I Classici Mondadori Fondazione Borletti), Milan (1949).
Mansi	J. D. Mansi, *Sacrorum conciliorum nova et amplissima collectio*, Florence–Venice (1759–98).
Michelet	Jules Michelet, *Documents inédits pour servir à l'histoire de France*, Paris (1840–51).
Migne PG	J. P. Migne, *Patrologiae cursus completus – Series graeca*, Paris (1857–66).
Migne PL	idem, *series latina*, Paris (1844–64).
Potthast	A. Potthast, *Regesta Pontificum Romanorum inde ab 1198 ad annum 1304*, Berlin (1873–75).
Ravaisson	Archives de la Bastille, *Documents inédits recueillis et publiés par François Ravaisson*, Paris (1866–1904).
Vogel	*Die Limburger Chronik.* ed. C. D. Vogel, Herborn (1826).

BIBLIOGRAPHY

We have listed only the relatively few general studies on our subject. Information about particular works on single periods and phenomena of the Satan cult can be found in the notes.

Baissac, Jules, *Les grands jours de la Sorcellerie*, Paris (1890).

Barney, Francis, *Prière à Satan – Messes noires d'hier et d'aujourd'hui*, Paris (1957).

Bois, Jules, *Le Satanisme et la Magie – avec une étude de J.-K. Huysmans*, Paris (1895, 1896).

Brévannes, Roland, *L'orgie satanique à travers les siècles*, Paris (1904).

Bricaud, Joanny, *La Messe Noire ancienne et moderne* (Bibliothèque Chacornac), Paris (1904).

Caufeynon et Jaf, Docteurs (pseudonyms), *Les Messes Noires, le culte de Satan-Dieu*, Paris (1905).

Legué, Gabriel, *La Messe noire*, Paris (1903).

Michelet, Jules, *La sorcière*. (First edition in two separate imprints, Paris (1862); see Refort, pp. VIIIff). Édition originale publiée avec notes et variantes par Lucien Refort (Société des textes Français Modernes), two vols., Paris (1952 and 1956).

In English: *The Witch of the Middle Ages*, translated by L. J. Trotter, London (1863); *Satanism and Witchcraft*, translated by A. R. Allinson, New York (1939).

Murray, Margaret Alice, *The God of the Witches*, London (1953).

Przybyszewski, Stanislaw, *Die Synagoge des Satan – Ihre Entstehung, Einrichtung und jetzige Bedeutung. Ein Versuch*, Berlin (1897).

Rhodes, Henry Taylor Fowkes, *The Satanic Mass*, London (1954), New York (1955).

Sylvius, Jehan, *Messes Noires. Satanisme et Luciférisme* (Collection 'Choses vues'), Paris (1929).

Villeneuve, Roland, *Le Diable. Érotologie de Satan* (Bibliothèque internationale d'érotologie No. 10) Paris (1963).

idem, 'Bibliographie démoniaque', in *Satan (Études Carmélitaines)*, pp. 647ff, Paris (1948).

Reference works

Plancy, Jacques Albin Simon, Collin de, *Dictionnaire infernal ou Répertoire universel des êtres, des personnages, etc.* First edition Paris (1818), Nouvelle édition entièrement refondue (1853), Paris (1863).

Robbins, Russell Hope, *The Encyclopedia of Witchcraft and Demonology*, New York (1959, 1960).

INDEX